Goya's Last Portrait /
A Question of Geography

Goya's Last Portrait / A Question of Geography

by

John Berger and Nella Bielski

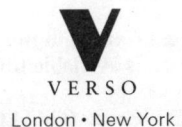

VERSO

London • New York

This omnibus edition first published by Verso 2026
Goya's Last Portrait first published by Faber and Faber Limited 1989
© John Berger and Nella Bielski 1989
A Question of Geography first published by Faber and Faber Limited 1987
© John Berger and Nella Bielski 1987

The manufacturer's authorized representative in the EU
for product safety (GPSR) is LOGOS EUROPE, 9 rue
Nicolas Poussin, 17000, La Rochelle, France
contact@logoseurope.eu

The moral rights of the authors have been asserted

1 3 5 7 9 10 8 6 4 2

Verso
UK: 6 Meard Street, London W1F 0EG
US: 207 East 32nd Street, New York, NY 10016
versobooks.com

Verso is the imprint of New Left Books

ISBN-13: 978-1-80429-877-0
ISBN-13: 978-1-80429-879-4 (US EBK)
ISBN-13: 978-1-80429-878-7 (UK EBK)

British Library Cataloguing in Publication Data
A catalogue record for this book is available from the British Library

Library of Congress Cataloging-in-Publication Data
A catalog record for this book is available from the Library of Congress

Printed and bound by CPI Group (UK) Ltd, Croydon, CR0 4YY

CONTENTS

GOYA'S LAST PORTRAIT: *The Painter Played Today*   1

A QUESTION OF GEOGRAPHY   107

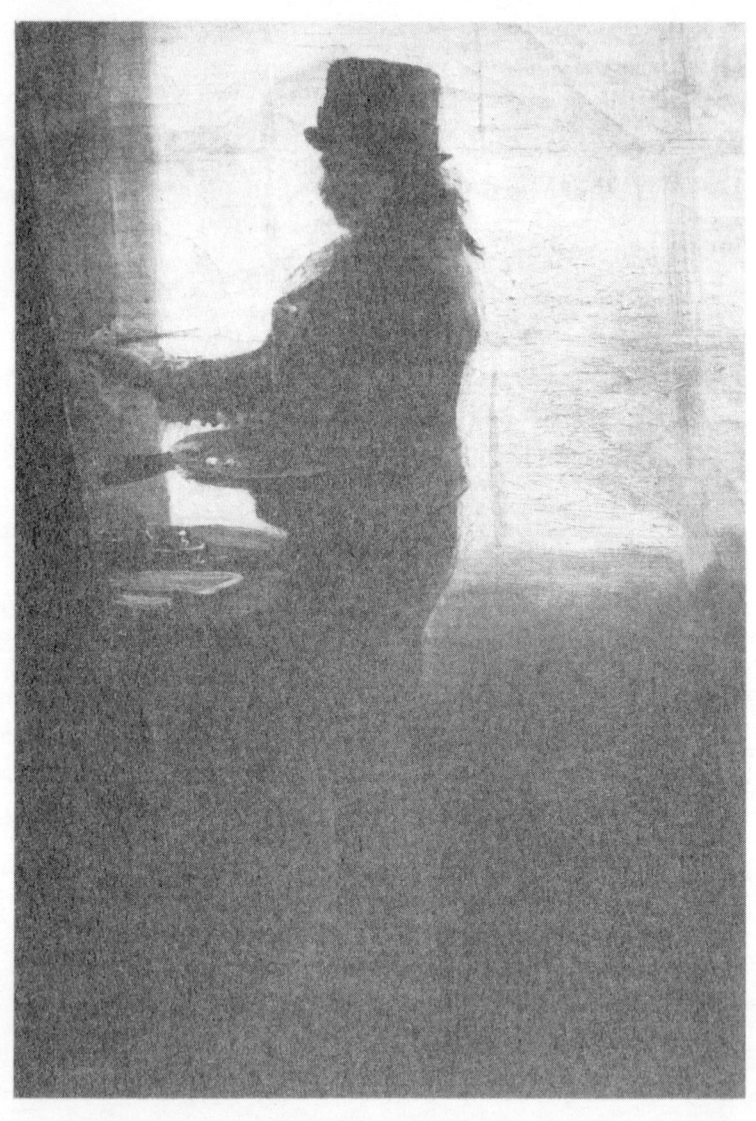

Self-Portrait (Conde de Villagonzalo, Madrid)

Goya's Last Portrait:
The Painter Played Today

For Tony Lyons in Madrid

CHARACTERS

GARDENER elderly
PEPA his daughter, early twenties
LEANDRO gardener's assistant, twenty-five
WIDOW sixty
DWARF a beggar, ageless
TONIO footballer, early thirties
FEDERICO Minister of Agriculture, fifty
ACTRESS twenty-five
DOCTOR fifty-five
GOYA

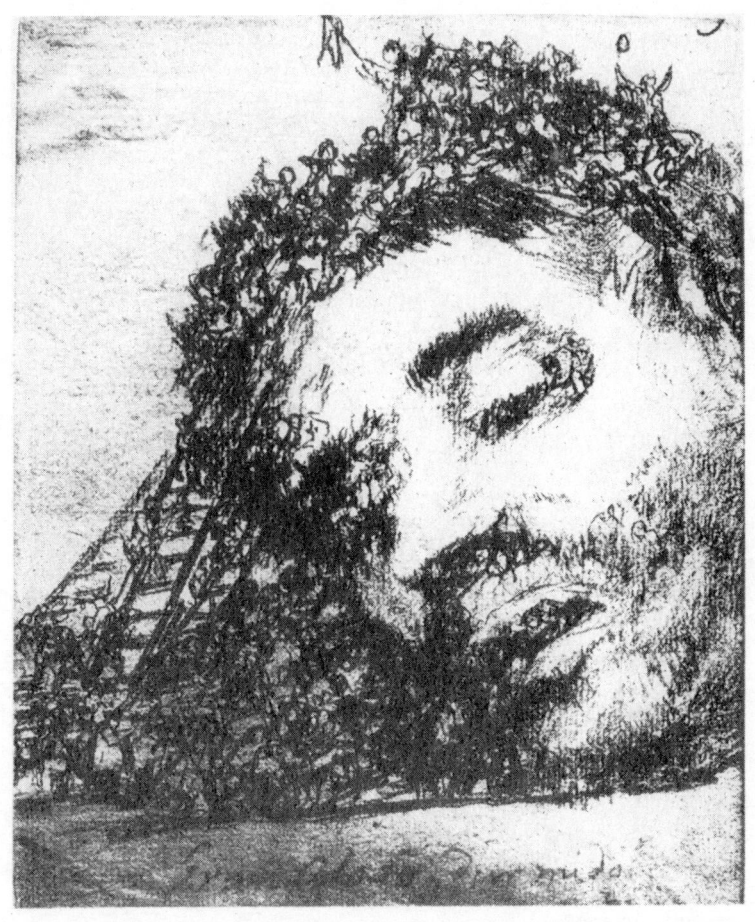

Sleeping giant
(drawing now destroyed)

*Late afternoon. Summer. The 1990s. A little-used corner of a cemetery
on a hill in Madrid. The tombs are overgrown. In the centre a ruin
which was once a chapel. Near left: door to the gardener's house. By
the door, a large bell. Far right: path leading to nearest gate of
cemetery. Near right: a* DWARF, *who is a professional beggar, sleeps
in the grass. In the ruined chapel a* WIDOW, *in black, is on her knees
murmuring the refrain of a prayer in Latin. Left: the elderly*
GARDENER, *masked and gloved, is bent over a beehive. Beside him,*
PEPA, *his daughter, is working a smoker to quieten the bees.*
LEANDRO, *a worker in the cemetery, crosses backstage carrying a coil
of hosepipe. He stops to look curiously at the two figures bent over the
hive.* PEPA *looks up, notices* LEANDRO *and waves. He returns the
greeting and walks off. Sound of a jet fighter in the sky.*

GARDENER: Every time one of their fucking F5s does that, I can't
    help thinking of the day when it won't be just an exercise.
PEPA: Leandro's taking me to a dance tonight.
GARDENER: Where?
PEPA: Near the Castellana.
GARDENER: You'll lose your job if you're late every morning.
    You'll be out of work. One of the millions. Look! Pepa!
    Look! There's the queen!
    (*Enter* ACTRESS, *accompanied by* DOCTOR.)
ACTRESS: (*To* DOCTOR) It's three years since I was here. I cannot
    tell you how much she fascinates me, this woman. Perhaps I
    should ask?
    (ACTRESS *approaches very tentatively and cautiously (because of
    her fear of bees)* GARDENER.)
    I wonder if you could tell me – we're looking for the grave of
    the Duchess of Alba.
    (GARDENER *raises his masked head but appears not to have
    understood.*)
GARDENER: In ten minutes the cemetery closes.
PEPA: You're on top of it. The Duchess of Alba's grave is the one

over there, the one where the stones have fallen.

(ACTRESS *and* DOCTOR *go to grave indicated backstage. They talk together, inaudible to us. Enter right* FEDERICO *and* TONIO, *two friends strolling through cemetery.* FEDERICO *wears a suit and carries a briefcase.* TONIO *is wearing jeans, canvas shoes and a white shirt.*)

FEDERICO: Anita used to bring me here when we were first going out together. Nothing's changed, it's so peaceful.

(*Re-enter* LEANDRO *who tentatively approaches the two men.*)

TONIO: I want to ask you a simple question. I see you so little these days. It's not a government secret.

LEANDRO: It can't be! Yet I know it is. It's him. Antonio Galvarez. I'd know him anywhere. Can I ask you, can I interrupt you for a second – could you give me your autograph?

(LEANDRO *offers* TONIO *an envelope.*)

The goal you saved in the last match against Lisbon, five minutes before the whistle . . . what a great save! Incredible!

TONIO: It's him you should ask for his autograph!

LEANDRO: Your friend?

TONIO: Yes. He's a minister in our government.

LEANDRO: I recognized you as soon as I saw you. It's Antonio Galvarez, I said. If it hadn't been for you we'd have lost against Lisbon! We all said the same . . . You were great. You had eyes in the palms of your hands. Could you sign on the back too? For my brother. Thank you.

(*Exit* LEANDRO. TONIO *and* FEDERICO *stroll on.*)

TONIO: Even in a cemetery they find me.

FEDERICO: Where more appropriate, my dear Tonio, than a cemetery? You're a popular hero!

(*Exit* FEDERICO *and* TONIO, *strolling, talking.*)

WIDOW: Grant him peace, O Lord, in thy mansions. Forgive him his sins, dear Lord, as I forgave him. He was short of breath and too fat, my poor Arturo. Coughed day and night. Yet he went on working to the end. Aceite de oliva, aceitunas, pimientos, cuanto señora? Ah yes! he said to the customers, if you want a healthy country, you have to look to the army! Punish him if you must, dear Lord, but only a little. He isn't

6

strong. Cut my toe-nails, Maria-Luisa, he used to say, I can't
reach them without you.

(DWARF *wakes up*.)

DWARF: Old lady takes a can
            To water her flowers
            Buried alive a man
            Will die of thirst

WIDOW: In your merciful goodness, O Lord, do not forsake your
humble servant, Maria-Luisa, and her poor son Felipe today
in jug. For stealing cars, dear Lord, cars. Even when he was
a toddler he liked everything mechanical. I know it wasn't
him. It's the company he keeps. Let a little justice come to
this earth, dear Lord.

(DWARF *approaches* WIDOW.)

DWARF: Merciful señora, consider my poverty and let my
wretchedness be a test of your virtue. Of the three, said the
Lord, the first is charity.

WIDOW: God gave you a head, a pair of legs and a pair of arms.
And your arms he gave you to work with!

DWARF: The rise in the standard of living, merciful señora, is bad
for us beggars. The more people have, the less they give. But
you, señora, I can see in your eyes – you are like a mother.

(PEPA *walks from beehive to bell and rings it. Re-enter* TONIO
and FEDERICO. *Everybody, except* GARDENER *and* PEPA,
*slowly takes the path to cemetery gate, and exits. As they do so we
hear snatches of their conversation*.)

WIDOW: (*To herself*) Let a little justice come to this earth, dear
Lord.

DOCTOR: (*To* ACTRESS) You wanted to seduce your father so you
became an actress.

TONIO: (*To* FEDERICO) It's something I ask myself in planes
when I have to fly . . . Are our civil wars over? Are they
impossible now?

DWARF: (*To* WIDOW) We have only a short time to please the
living, all eternity to please the dead.

LEANDRO: (*Shouting to* PEPA) Wear your new white dress tonight!
(*When all have gone, another jet fighter crosses the sky*.)

GARDENER: They are filling the second honey box; it'll be a good

7

year, Pepa. Do you know how . . . ?

PEPA: Yes, Papa, I know. You tell me every July.

(*Enter* LEANDRO *and* ACTRESS, *running from the direction of the cemetery gate. They are agitated.*)

LEANDRO: Not a drop of rain!

ACTRESS: I saw it but I don't know what it is!

LEANDRO: It goes as far as the horizon on every side.

ACTRESS:How can such a thing happen?

(*Enter* WIDOW.)

WIDOW: It's the end of the world.

(*Enter* FEDERICO *and* TONIO, *followed by* DOCTOR.)

FEDERICO: With a blue sky, without a sound, within half an hour.

ACTRESS: One of you, for Christ's sake, one of you tell me how such a thing can happen?

DOCTOR: In principle such a transformation takes several hundred millennia.

GARDENER: My God! They've done it! They've ruined the world.

(GARDENER, WIDOW *and* TONIO *kneel.*)

FEDERICO: God won't help us.

GARDENER: There were so many warnings.

LEANDRO: I'm going to build us a raft.

(*Enter* GOYA, *dressed in a frogman suit, from direction of cemetery gate. With his appearance the mood changes. He is dripping wet. Takes off mask. A man in his forties.*)

FEDERICO: Where have you come from?

GOYA: From Fuendetodos.

ACTRESS: Fuendetodos? On what planet is that?

GOYA: On this one.

ACTRESS: How did you manage to get here?

(GOYA *mimes swimming.*)

TONIO: You're saying the water goes as far as Saragossa?

(GOYA *nods.*)

FEDERICO: Salt?

(GOYA *nods.*)

WIDOW: It's not possible. With the feet of the Devil himself, you couldn't have swum from Saragossa to Madrid! How many kilometres is it?

LEANDRO: Four hundred and twenty-seven. I've done it on my
motor bike.

WIDOW: No!

DWARF: If he says he did, he did.

GOYA: I come here every evening. But for you, all of you, to be
here together, I've waited a hundred and sixty years.

ACTRESS: That makes him a ghost!

DOCTOR: Collective hallucinations, my dear, are a phenomenon
I've written a paper on.

ACTRESS: Who are you?

GOYA: I made a lot of money out of my heads. I was the father of
many children, nineteen, twenty, I forget. And I was famous
among the Cuadrillas.

WIDOW: God in heaven! It's him. My Chico. Only Chico could
invent such stories. Nobody in Fuendetodos believed him.

GOYA: Nobody in Fuendetodos believed anything, madre.

ACTRESS: Are you her son? Is she really your mother?

WIDOW: How dare you suggest he's not my child!

GOYA: I'm her son, yes. And I'm your lover.

ACTRESS: How would you paint me?

GOYA: Lying on your back, legs crossed. Your eyes looking into
mine.

ACTRESS: Dressed?

GOYA: For those who wish.

ACTRESS: Undressed! Coward.

GOYA: Get rid of her!

ACTRESS: It wasn't then that you said that!

GOYA: Sometimes I forget the order of things.

FEDERICO: You had a sense of timing, Francisco, like none of us.
The moments burnt you or you burnt them. But you had no
sense of history. You remember when I came to ask your
help?

GOYA: How did I reply?

FEDERICO: You refused me and I spent years in jail.

GOYA: I don't remember.

TONIO: I never doubted for an instant you'd come in the end.

GOYA: I've come to see my mother.

TONIO: I thought your mother was dead.

9

GOYA: A mere detail.

PEPA: That's exactly what you said. In Saragossa. The year before I was born.

GOYA: I was very old when I met you.

PEPA: On Friday at 2 p.m. in the Place d'Aquitaine, there will be a public execution, French style.

GOYA: I shall be there.

PEPA: A poor wretch called Jean Bertain murdered his brother-in-law.

GOYA: So many murders . . . I remember nothing about Jean Bertain.

DOCTOR: I would like to ask you a medical question –

GOYA: No, I didn't have the clap.

DOCTOR: You often complained of a sense of water filling your head. A kind of aquaphobia. Your role as a frogman is perhaps a compensation.

GOYA: That's your business . . .

DOCTOR: My question is this: did your aquaphobia precede your deafness or follow it?

(GOYA *ignores the question.*)

GARDENER: (*Referring to* DOCTOR) It was he, Don Francisco, who stole your skull.

GOYA: I know, I know. What difference does it make, one skull more or less? I can live without a skull. I belong to the twentieth century, they say. I was born in the eighteenth. Everything is mixed . . . There's a child crying, I see soldiers raping a woman, I hear interrogations under torture . . . Two centuries ago a Dutchman painted a goldfinch. That's true isn't it, Pepa?

PEPA: For us it's four centuries ago today.

LEANDRO: (*Jealous*) Who is this man?

PEPA: Francisco de Goya y Lucientes.

GOYA: Francisco de Goya y Lucientes . . . What is it? I still don't know . . .

FEDERICO: OK, Paco, OK. I know your jokes by heart. You've trapped us here with your trick flood. But now let's come down to earth. Be reasonable. (*He looks at his watch.*) In exactly one hour I've a meeting with the Prime Minister.

10

Life must go on. It was a good joke, Paco . . .

GOYA: A good joke! What the hell! What the hell, my friends! All my life, what the hell my loved ones, I was haunted . . . Today you use my name whenever you want to say haunted, whenever you want to say living in a hell. Goyaesque, my arse! You live in your century and I'm in peace everlasting, this is how you think. What the hell! I've trapped you here this evening and I'm going to put you to work. The tables are turned, tonight the tables are turned. You spectators are going to make my portrait. You're going to begin immediately. You're going to paint me with your lives. Prime ministers or no prime ministers, dances or no dances. You are going to do my portrait for me, painted with your bodies and souls. So I can see myself at last and then die. So I can forget Francisco de Goya y Lucientes for ever!

GARDENER: What colour ground shall I prepare for the canvas, Don Francisco?

GOYA: White. Blinding white.

(*White curtain descends.*)

11

ACT ONE

SCENE I

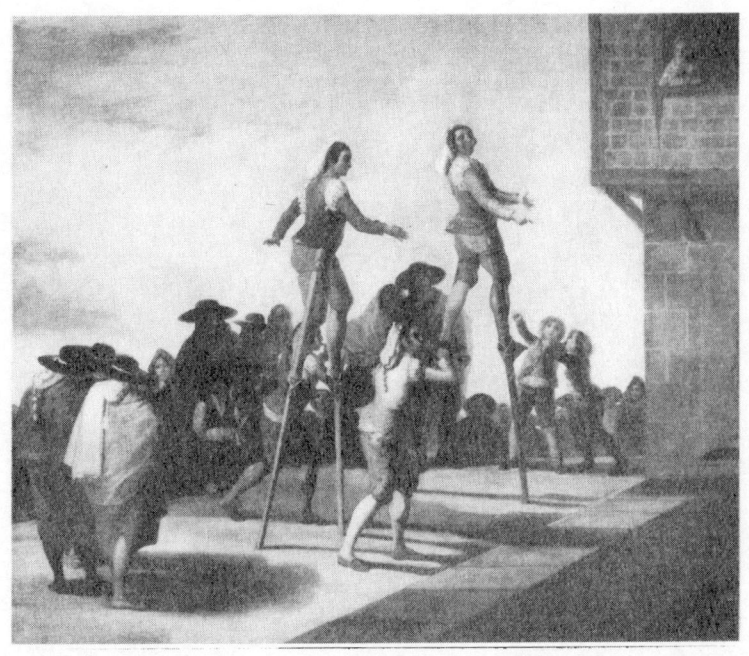

The stilt-walkers
(The Prado, Madrid)

*Front of stage before semi-transparent curtain, through which cemetery
is partially visible. Chair, dressing-table, open trunk of clothes.*
ACTRESS *is dressing and making up as* DUCHESS.

ACTRESS: I can't get him out of my head, he's there. Francisco de
Goya y Lucientes. When I want to mock him I shall call him
Frogman. How is it possible that I, Doña Cayetana, with my
beauty, my taste, my name – can't get him out of my head?
He pursues me as no man has ever done. When he leaves me,
he stays there. He's small, short-legged, plump, getting on in
age. Worst of all, he's married, father of God knows how
many children. How is it possible? Anyway I intend to live
either with or without him! And I'm going to show you all
who the Duchess of Alba is!
(*Curtain goes up to reveal autumn night. Garden of one of the
Duchess of Alba's residences near Madrid. Chinese lanterns. The
scene is basically that of the cemetery – as is the case throughout
the entire play. Beside the ruined chapel a brand-new horse
carriage with white wheels. An English phaeton. The* DWARF,
dressed as the bufón (*jester) of the Duchess's household, is
standing near the carriage.* ACTRESS, *now* DUCHESS, *wanders
across stage.*)
DUCHESS: En France, ils font la révolution. Il ne faut pas rater ça!
(DUCHESS *exits towards the house and the music.*)
DWARF: There's no country in the world funnier than ours. We
have tribunals which hang twenty citizens a day and
afterwards argue for twenty years about the best way of
unharnessing a mule from a cart. (*He glances at carriage.*)
Comedy is everywhere. As the great nation of conquistadors
who converted the southern continent of America, the oceans
are always with us. We have fifteen ships in the Royal Navy.
And for these fifteen ships we have one Grand Admiral, two
Admirals, twenty-nine Vice-Admirals, sixty-three Second
Vice-Admirals and two hundred and fourteen ship's captains!

15

(*Enter* DUCHESS *holding a flaming torch, accompanied by*
DOCTOR, FEDERICO, GARDENER, TONIO. *All but* GARDENER
are dressed as courtiers.)
We are a nation of rags and uniforms.
(DWARF *opens carriage door.* GOYA (*in his mid-forties*),
elegantly dressed as court painter, steps out.)
This man paints the uniforms. The uniforms adore it.
(GOYA *crosses the stage to kiss* DUCHESS's *hand. She withdraws
it quickly, majestically, and advances to the footlights; the*
DOCTOR *following behind her. She addresses the public.*)

DUCHESS: The Jacobins are insisting upon a trial for Louis and
Marie-Antoinette. They will be executed . . . for us, with our
experience, this is a foregone conclusion. I too would like to
be executed. The head is severed and the name is
remembered for ever.

GOYA: Cayetana!

DUCHESS: I have not yet given the word. Monarchs order their
own executions, although to the ignorant it appears
otherwise. Tonight the Thirteenth Duchess of Alba has
come to a decision and you are assembled here to be the first
to hear it. (*Aside to* DOCTOR) Are you sure the servants are
ready? (*To public*) The century into which we were born is
waning to its close. The Royal Observatory is being built so
that men can look at the night sky through telescopes. A
woman has no need of a telescope. Doña Maria Teresa
Cayetana de Silva y Alvarez de Toledo can already see the
new century approaching. The nineteenth it will be called.
'The nineteenth century.' The sound is awkward. An
indivisible number. The twentieth sounds better.

DWARF: (*Tapping carriage*) Fucking Phaeton Silver Shadow!

DUCHESS: Perhaps in the twenty-second century, with a 2 beside
a 2, the impossible will become possible and we'll open like
flowers, again and again and again . . . (*To* DWARF) Would
you like to live, Amore, in a time when no flower ever fades?
(*To* DOCTOR) It's better that you go and supervise them. I
want the flames well timed.
(*Exit* DOCTOR.)
Tonight the Thirteenth Duchess of Alba has an

announcement to make to you. She is going to give everything away. Everything she has inherited is to become yours. This land, her forest, the game in the forests –

GOYA: She's out of her mind, game is for kings, not peasants.

DUCHESS: – her sheep and horses, her mills and fountains, her presses and fruit trees, her vines and coach houses, everything, her entire estate she is giving to you before you suffer the shame of having to ask for it, before you become a mob, unaware of what you're taking. Doña Maria Teresa Cayetana de Silva y Alvarez de Toledo, Thirteenth Duchess of Alba, offers to you herewith, her one-time servitors and tenants, the patrimony of her family in Castile. Take it with her blessing!

(*Enter* DOCTOR *hurriedly.*)

DOCTOR: (*Confidentially to* DUCHESS) The servants are refusing!

DUCHESS: Then whip them!

DOCTOR: I warned you they'd refuse.

FEDERICO: As if history was a child you could teach! (*To* GOYA) Your Cayetana lives on another planet.

GOYA: I've been there!

DUCHESS: (*Turning to* DWARF) Amore, what would you like to see burnt?

DWARF: The dresses of all the brides in the world!

DUCHESS: Why?

DWARF: So I can see what otherwise I'll never see.

DUCHESS: (*To public*) Guests, the Duchess of Alba demands one last service of you. Come with her to set fire to her palace. That all burn! Rooms, galleries, library, beds, tapestries, portraits!

(GOYA *hurries out.*)

That all burn! Linen, velvets, brocades, lace, silks. All the crap of this vanity of a life, let it burn! Chests, closets, carriages, coffers. That all burn! And that we, watching, be purified and proud of how we faced the end of our time together!

(*Enter* GOYA *carrying a large framed portrait* (*we do not see the painting*), *which he places carefully in his carriage.*)

Why is there no cheering?

17

TONIO: It's premature, Doña Cayetana, too soon.

DUCHESS: I want to see it burn.

TONIO: It can't happen yet.

DUCHESS: I will insist.

TONIO: If you insist, they will kill you first.

(*Enter* DOCTOR.)

DOCTOR: They're filling sacks with sand to put out any fire. They're carrying water on their heads from the well.

DUCHESS: (*To* TONIO) You, Don Antonio, who know so much, tell me why.

TONIO: The madness hasn't come from them.

DUCHESS: I'm giving them everything!

DWARF: It's Tuesday, Doña Cayetana, and on Tuesdays there's no more crime in Madrid. No thieving, no rape, no murder. Not even, Doña Cayetana, a single case of arson.

DUCHESS: I want to see it burn, Amore.

DWARF: Every Tuesday the Devil goes to Paris – to dine with Robespierre. Try it next on a Friday, Doña Cayetana, a Friday or a Monday.

(*Exit* DUCHESS, *accompanied by* DWARF, DOCTOR.)

GARDENER: (*To* GOYA) She's shrewd, your lady. She was testing public opinion, I could see; trying it on. Fortunately no one reacted. Fortunately we live in a time of peace.

FEDERICO: Peace! The Inquisition promises peace to the souls of the bodies they torture!

(FEDERICO *walks to sit on a tomb backstage.* GARDENER *crosses stage, opens door of carriage, takes out a pot of paint and brush and, sitting on the ground, starts to paint one of the white wheels white.* GOYA *addresses* TONIO.)

GOYA: (*Running his hand along the coachwork*) English. Shipped to Barcelona in pieces and assembled in Madrid. I paid eight thousand reales for it. He's my coachman. I brought him to Madrid. He was born in Fuendetodos like me. We grazed goats together. He understands horses and mules as well. Whilst Juan drives, I lie back on the upholstery, which smells of limes and sherry, and I gently lift the mantilla off her head.

TONIO: Cayetana's hair –

18

GOYA: 'The Duchess of Alba', Tonio, would sound better from
your lips.

TONIO: You've no need to worry, Francisco, she doesn't take me
seriously. She listens to my advice about certain things, but I
count no more than Amore the Dwarf, or Rodriguez the
Doctor or the violinist her husband. If I speak of what's in
my heart, she mocks me: 'Who do you take me for, Don
Antonio? A turtle dove? Consider me, my friend, with a
different eye.' If I had a little of your genius, Francisco . . .

GOYA: Genius! God forbid! Genius is a calamity. A catastrophe.
Something you fall into – like Paul on the road to Damascus.
Brilliance! Skill! Cunning! Speed! They're words I like to
hear and words I'm used to hearing. In any case she's right,
she's no turtle dove. She flies by night and she keeps strange
company.

(*Enter* DWARF, *who has been hiding behind a tree.*)

DWARF: A moth with white stockings and a ring on her finger
inscribed with the letter – the letter F!

GOYA: One day they'll burn you, Amore.

DWARF: Show its pair! Show the ring on the middle finger of your
left hand! (DWARF *tries to seize* GOYA'*s hand.*)

GOYA: Do you want me to throw you over the cemetery wall?

(FEDERICO *approaches the others.*)

FEDERICO: The tension mounts! Do you never stop playing? And
at your age, Francisco! I've something to tell you which is a
little more prosaic. Agents of the Holy Office entered my
house and searched my library yesterday morning. Tidy,
systematic, correct. They took away 231 books. I counted
those which were missing. It may have been 233. I'm
assuming that two of the books were ones I lent to a student
and I'm not sure whether he returned them. They also left
me a warning.

GOYA: What did it say, the warning?

FEDERICO: *French science corrupts*. It's just the beginning. Luis de
Samaniego has been arrested and flung into prison. Every
scrap of news which comes from Paris means they'll pull the
net tighter. Unhappily it's not the Duchess's theatre that'll
save us. Are you driving back to the city tonight? Perhaps

19

you could take me?
(GOYA *opens door of carriage and bows.* FEDERICO, TONIO *and* GOYA *enter carriage and close door.* GARDENER *continues to paint wheel white. Lights fade, darkness.*)

ACT ONE

SCENE 2

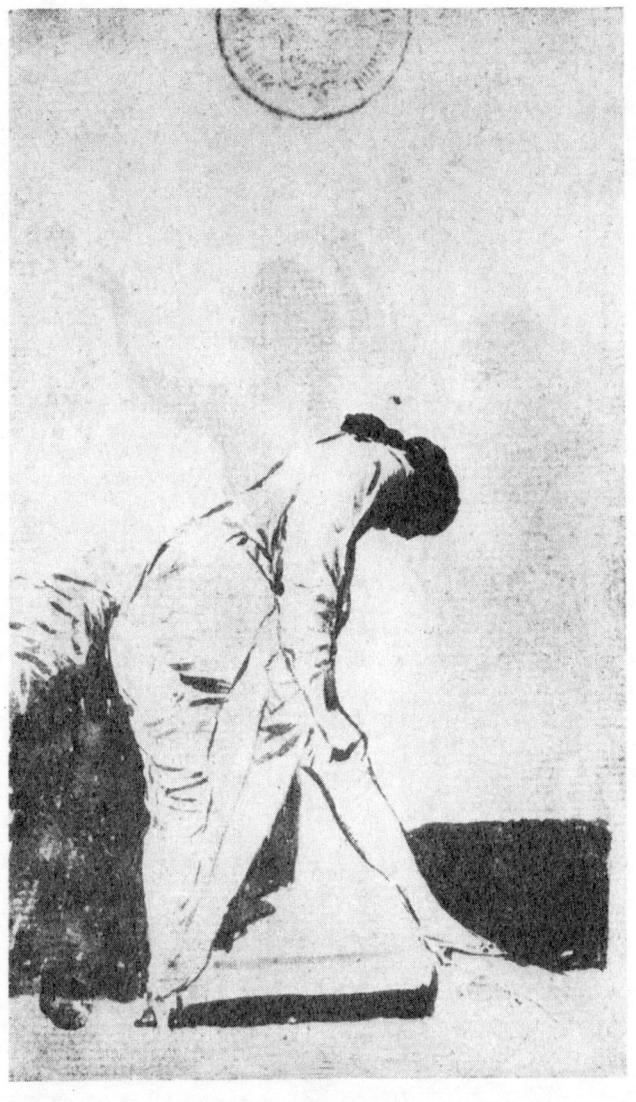

The garter
(The Prado, Madrid)

Same as previous scene except that the Chinese lanterns have been extinguished. It is the middle of the night. Total silence. DWARF *with lantern is alone on stage.*

DWARF: Comedy everywhere, day and night. Our King is known as the He-Goat. He likes shooting partridges. So does Goya. They do it together. The difference between the He-Goat and Goya is that Goya is frightened of being cuckolded and the He-Goat doesn't mind. The Queen is called the Whore. She doesn't mind this, but if some unfortunate calls her the Toothless Whore, he or she is thrown into prison. A special branch of the Holy Office deals exclusively with this seditious nuance. The Prime Minister, who is the Whore's lover, is referred to throughout the land as the Blood Sausage. Somebody has arrived.

(DWARF *opens the carriage door and* GOYA, *wearing a hat with lit candles around the brim, gets out.* DUCHESS *enters, running, dressed in white.* DWARF *places lantern on ground and exits.*)

DUCHESS: There you are! Lit up! I scratched myself on the thorns running, in the dark. My foot touched a snake. I was waiting for you.

GOYA: For how many nights?

DUCHESS: Nobody asks me such a question. Your duty was to arrive.

GOYA: I'm here.

DUCHESS: What makes a man fight a duel?

GOYA: Honour.

DUCHESS: Foolish. Honour is nothing.

GOYA: If you were a man, you would never fight a duel?

DUCHESS: Perhaps.

GOYA: If not for honour, for what?

DUCHESS: So as to understand you . . . Approach you . . . Come closer to you.

(GOYA *places hat with candles on ground.*)

23

How are you going to come through the thicket of thorns?

GOYA: With my eyes open and my face unprotected.

DUCHESS: What will you do with Cleopatra's two asps?

GOYA: I will entwine them together to make a necklace for the Duchess of Alba.

DUCHESS: How far will you go?

GOYA: To the last stitch and the last wound.

(DUCHESS *pinches out candles.*)

DUCHESS: What will cure you?

GOYA: Your weight on my shoulders.

DUCHESS: Where will you carry me?

GOYA: To Fuendetodos.

(*Scarcely visible in the light of the lantern, the two figures approach the carriage. Lantern goes out. Total darkness.*)

DUCHESS: When I die, I will give you the flour of my bones, my Arab legs and my name for ever.

(*Noise of carriage door shutting. Violently all lights go full up. No one is to be seen inside the carriage or out. Even the lantern has disappeared.*)

ACT ONE

SCENE 3

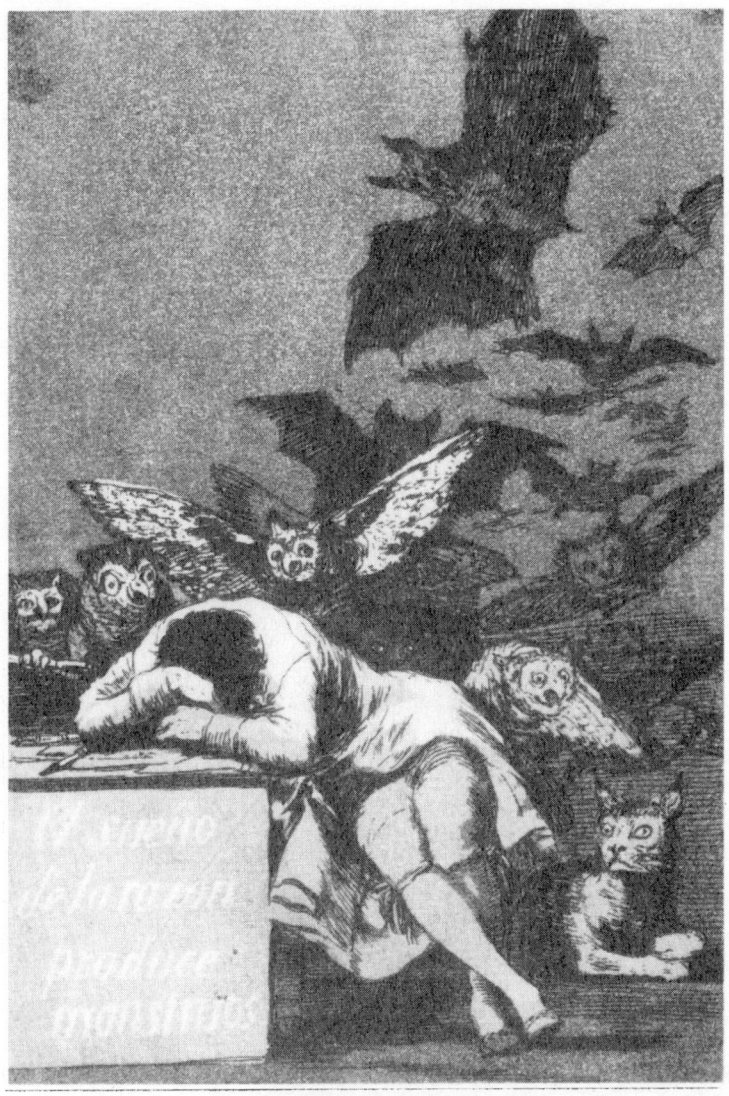

The Sleep of Reason Begets Monsters
(The British Museum)

*A few weeks later. Goya's house in Madrid. Front of stage before
semi-transparent curtain through which cemetery is dimly visible.*
FEDERICO *seated at table.* GOYA *standing, holding a handful of
papers.*

GOYA: I have too many commissions, there's the problem. I'm
looking for a good assistant, can't find one. People don't
know how to paint any more. Too stiff, no flexibility. You
have to be like a brush to be a painter. Like a sable in the
forest. Flexibility is all . . . think of José Garcia (*Imitates
bullfighter*) – there's an artist.
FEDERICO: I've come to ask your help.
GOYA: How much do you need? Is it to pay the printers? There
are men whose destiny is to owe money to poor printers all
their lives. They are creatures who can't stop writing and
who can't write what the authorities want! Isn't that so?
FEDERICO: No, this time it's not that.
GOYA: What have you written now? Another report on the state of
our peasantry? The poverty of our villages? The reluctance
with which we relinquish the dying? Ah, my dear Federico,
in another life you'll have a great political following.
FEDERICO: In this one now I have some.
GOYA: I know, I know, you fight like a lion for justice, for the
good of the people . . .
FEDERICO: I need your help.
GOYA: How many reales? I'm expecting a packet any day now. A
commission from Her Majesty the Whore. She wanted the
whole family done. All the royal meat, from the infantas to
the ga-gas, shimmering pink through lace and silk. They
were delighted. So was I. Yet how it hurts them to pay! It
makes me laugh. Listen to this, an account from the King's
Exchequer. 'Concerning your payment, we are, I take it, in
agreement: six heads at 2000 reales apiece, and five heads at
1000. As you will observe I have counted therein the head of

27

His Highness the Baby Prince. But, as I'm sure you will concur, heads number 12 and number 13 of the other royal children who were absent should not be included, any more than head number 14 which is a portrait of yourself . . .'

FEDERICO: Lending me money you risk nothing.

GOYA: No need to reassure me.

FEDERICO: What I have come to ask you does involve a risk.

GOYA: You want me to paint you something in secret, something it would be unwise to show to others? You're not the first, my friend, and I'm an expert. Discreet, skilful, subtle. I have several secret pictures of my own. We live in such times. Nobody has seen them. Nobody will find them. Tell me what the subject is?

FEDERICO: Neither money nor paintings, Francisco. For once it concerns flesh and blood. And a brain. A brain they want to stop working. I need to hide for a few days.

GOYA: Where?

FEDERICO: Here in your house.

GOYA: When?

FEDERICO: Now. They're searching for me.

GOYA: The Holy Office?

FEDERICO: Yes, the Inquisition.

GOYA: Too many people come to this house. It would be dangerous.

FEDERICO: For a few days where you hide your secret pictures . . . Time to let Romero spread the rumour I've left for Lisbon. Then we'll arrange that 'somebody' see me in Lisbon.

GOYA: If I didn't have an official position . . .

FEDERICO: A few months ago we all had official positions –

GOYA: An official position in the King's Household.

FEDERICO: We're losing them one by one. Luis de Samaniego has been tortured. Since then, no news. Silence.

GOYA: Our crime? What is it? We believe in Reason. We believe Reason is given to man.

FEDERICO: They believe in the garrote and the sambenito.

GOYA: Better to die than the sambenito.

FEDERICO: Jovellanos and Saavedra have been forced into exile.

GOYA: Are they already investigating me? Do you suppose I'm being watched?

FEDERICO: Luis de Samaniego taught mathematics in the University of Salamanca. No less innocent than painting canvases, at first glance, no less innocent.

GOYA: Take the carriage. Let me offer you my carriage. With it you can make your getaway.

FEDERICO: Like carriage – like man!

GOYA: What do you mean?

FEDERICO: Both are too conspicuous. No, don't protest. I haven't a minute to lose. I've lost time here already.

(FEDERICO *grasps* GOYA's *arm and walks swiftly off. Stops and turns round at last moment.*)

I've never presumed to give you advice about your art, but since we may not see each other for a long time, remember what I say now. You must use another medium. Less conspicuous. Easier to hide. Unofficial. With which one can make several copies in case some are lost. For some are always lost. Adieu, Francisco.

ACT ONE

SCENE 4

Sketch of nude
(The Prado, Madrid)

Day. Spring (1794). Duchess's residence. To right of chapel a bed
with muslin hangings. DUCHESS *bent over bed murmuring.*
GARDENER *painting wheel of carriage.* GOYA *opens carriage door,*
climbs down. GARDENER *stops painting. Both men watch* DUCHESS
who continues her ministrations to sick child in bed.

DUCHESS: Going away, going away, soon there'll be no pain left,
    I'll take it all away. Don't fret, give it to me, little one . . .
GARDENER: If she had a child of her own – the Duke, they say, is
    not a breeding animal.
DUCHESS: Sip, darling, from the lemons of our very own garden.
GOYA: Nobody on earth should be allowed to have a voice like
    hers.
DUCHESS: Did you dream the world was bad? No, no, only theirs,
    not ours. It's cooling – if I press it against you – see – it cools,
    it cools my honey.
GOYA: It's so beautiful, it cuts your throat from ear to ear, a voice
    like hers.
DUCHESS: There, the hurt is coming, come to me, come to me,
    we'll mend everything, feather by feather . . . come, little
    pain, come to Cayetana, come, little death.
GOYA: My mother used to say death was a feather.
GARDENER: Your mother, Don Francisco, is a woman who
    weighs her words.
DUCHESS: Don't come too close, both of you. Not too close. His
    eyes are closed.
GARDENER: The swallowing disease?
DUCHESS: Peace.
GOYA: Scarlet fever?
GARDENER: The illness of the marshes?
GOYA: Typhoid?
    (DWARF *leaps up, tears down hangings and jumps out of bed.*)
DWARF: Growing pains!
    (GOYA, *seized with a fit of rage, swears at the* GARDENER.)

DUCHESS: Why are you so angry? Come and sit beside me. Let us say good day to each other. Good day, Frogman.

GOYA: How does your husband put up with that creature?

DUCHESS: My husband puts up with nothing. He plays Haydn.

GOYA: And I put up with everything.

DUCHESS: Don't you think others have the right to play jokes? Does every caprice have to be signed by the master on a plate?

GARDENER: My God! Do you hear what she says! You've shown her, haven't you? You've shown her. How many times have I told you to show nobody? It's dangerous for nineteen reasons.

DUCHESS: Baturros! Baturros! You don't know how to live. Neither of you even knows the difference between a coachman and master. Listen how he talks to you.

GOYA: (*To* GARDENER) She has only seen one or two donkeys.

GARDENER: And the donkey is who? Twenty reasons. Have you ever heard anybody ever stop talking here? Never. Prattle! The Devil needs nothing more.

DUCHESS: And in Aragon, sir?

GARDENER: In Aragon, Your Duchess, men measure their words, use them sparingly and keep them.

(GOYA *makes friendly sign to* GARDENER, *who returns to carriage, picks up paint pot, gets in, shuts door.*)

DUCHESS: Are you still angry? I have arranged something special for you.

GOYA: More theatre with the Dwarf?

DUCHESS: Do you know why I call him Amore?

GOYA: I killed a man once.

DUCHESS: I've never met a man who hasn't boasted of killing another. Even my husband says he killed a man . . . a flautist it seems. No more need for anger. I want to show you something.

(GARDENER *pulls down blind of carriage window.* DUCHESS *enters the ruined chapel, followed by* GOYA. *Silence. We do not see the painting they are looking at.*)

DUCHESS: I acquired it at the age of thirteen when I got married.

GOYA: He was impervious. He judged nothing. He kept his

34

eternal distance. Only his glance caresses her.

DUCHESS: His glance! What does his glance matter? There's a woman there, lying on a bed, naked. I watch her every night after my prayers. It's she who counts.

GOYA: For very little, she counts for very little. Look at the draperies which echo and enclose her body. He knew exactly what he was doing.

DUCHESS: She counts for very little! Your impudence! You peer at us, you get a cunning kick out of pinning us with your brushes to your sheets, your canvases and then you boast: He knew exactly what he was doing! You know nothing. Men see only surfaces, only appearances. Incorrigibly stiff, incorrigibly rigid, the lot of you! Male monuments to your everlasting erections!

GOYA: I could do better.

DUCHESS: I could do better! Nothing else matters. Maria Teresa Cayetana de Silva y Alvarez de Toledo has shown her Velázquez, the only naked woman reclining on a bed painted in the long history of Spanish art, to her lover who is a painter and what does he say: 'I could do better.'

GOYA: I could do better.

DUCHESS: How would you paint me?

GOYA: Lying on your back, legs crossed. Your eyes looking into mine.

DUCHESS: Dressed?

GOYA: For those who wish.

DUCHESS: Undressed! Coward!

GOYA: First dressed!

DUCHESS: What patience! What restraint.

GOYA: Next, in the twinkling of an eye, undressed.

DUCHESS: With my consent.

GOYA: With your consent, Cayetana, or without it. I can tear off your clothes. I can strip you as well as I can paint you. Here! (*He points to his head.*) That's where I have an edge over Velázquez. No mirrors. I advance on my stomach. Mix my colours with spunk.

DUCHESS: Your colours, sir, are your business. It will be done from memory. You will paint me when you are alone. You will remember all the women you have known, all the women you have stripped – as you so eloquently put it – you will close your eyes and see them again and then you will use all your effort, all your virility, all your speed to recall what distinguishes every square centimetre of the body of the Thirteenth Duchess of Alba from the body of any other woman now or hereafter. From memory. It will be a solitary proof of your love . . . Afterwards I promise you a month in the country . . . the two of us together.

(GARDENER *climbs out of carriage, starts painting wheel*. GOYA *crosses stage*.)

GOYA: More and more and more and more . . . brazen!

(GOYA *enters carriage*. DUCHESS *waves a handkerchief*.)

DUCHESS: Work fast, Frogman.

(*Lights fade*.)

ACT ONE

SCENE 5

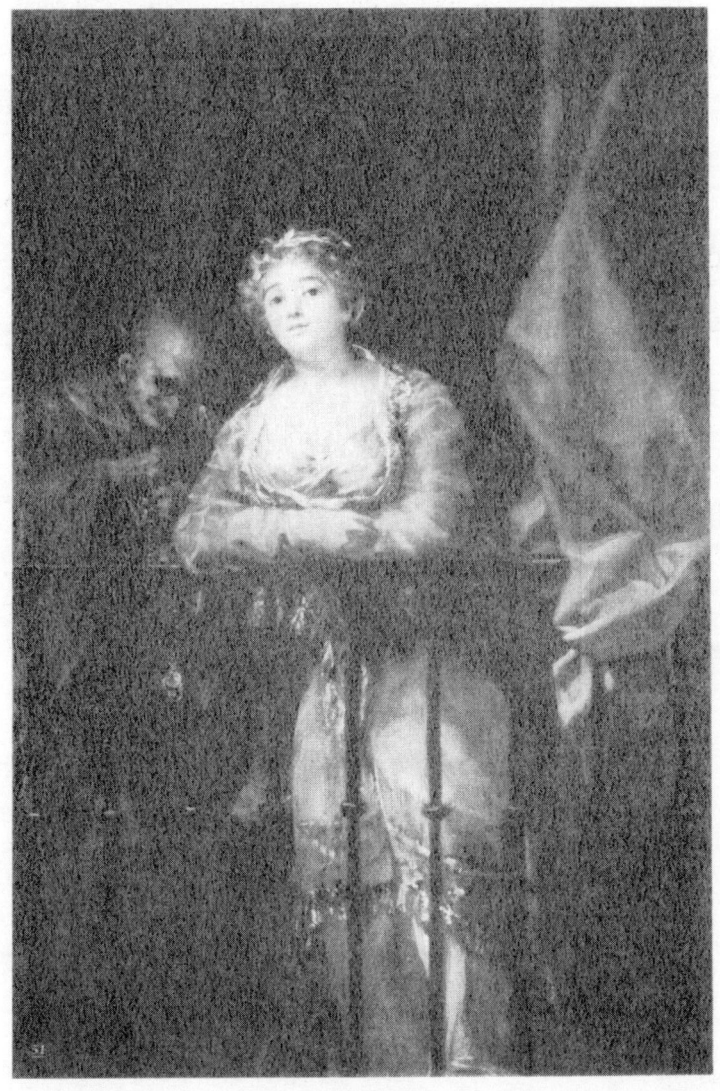

Maja and Celeste on balcony
(Private collection, Madrid)

Summer evening (1794). An inn in the countryside. Table and chairs.
PEPA, *dressed as a servant, is slumped in a chair, idle. Voice of*
GARDENER *offstage.*

GARDENER: If we drive any further in this shit, it'll be up to the
    axles. With your lady nothing is simple, Francisco, nothing.
    *(From behind the chapel appears an enormous bouquet of roses –
    as if advancing by itself.* PEPA *stares, mesmerized.* GARDENER,
    *hidden by the flowers he is carrying, picks his way forward,
    followed by* GOYA *carrying a chest.)*
    We want a room with a window that looks out on to a
    pomegranate tree.
    *(*PEPA *does not react.)*
GOYA: You have a room on the first floor with a balcony. Almost
    touching the balcony is a pomegranate tree. That is the room
    I want.
PEPA: The third room, yes, with a pomegranate tree outside. It's
    always the first choice. You're lucky, for no one else has
    come tonight.
    *(*GOYA *opens the chest, and takes out some embroidered silk.)*
GOYA: Hang this by the window – a little to the side, so. These
    pillows *(Takes out lace pillows.)* for the bed. And be quick
    about it.
PEPA: What are we going to do with the flowers? There are not
    enough vases in the whole inn.
GARDENER: Then wet a sheet and give me that.
PEPA: I'll ask Uncle.
    (Exit PEPA.)
GARDENER: If her taste for roses doesn't slow down, we're going
    to need a dozen more gardens.
GOYA: Do I owe you money?
GARDENER: Money . . . money. You're ruining yourself,
    Francisco. You're heading for catastrophe. It's costing too
    much this passion of yours. It's not like your Phaeton. You

39

buy a Phaeton and it's yours, for good. With her . . . Soon
there will be no more heads left for you to paint. Do you
realize that? Everybody who can afford it will have been
painted by you.

GOYA: You'll see, Juan. From now on I'm going to paint only
roses.

(*Enter* PEPA *with two massive oil jars.*)

PEPA: My uncle suggested these . . .

GOYA: Perfect. You arrange the flowers, Juan. We haven't time to
waste. Bring some fruit – peaches, melons – and some wine.
Black.

PEPA: Nothing more to eat?

GOYA: She eats nothing. She has the appetite of a small bird.

GARDENER: (*To himself*) Birds eat continually. They never stop.
She's devouring him to the last morsel.

PEPA: (*To* GARDENER) And for you, sir? You look as if a plate of
potatoes and bacon would go down well.

GOYA: No time for eating.

PEPA: You are all the same when you make your rendezvous here.
Not a moment to be lost! She's coming! She's coming! And
the moments go by . . . and the hours . . . she's never in a
hurry. The other day there was a gentleman – come to think
of it he also asked for the room with the pomegranate tree –
he comes for a night, and he stays for a week waiting.

GOYA: Who was he?

PEPA: A student from Madrid, nice looking, much younger than
you, slim, with curly hair.

GOYA: What happened?

PEPA: He arrives and he says he's waiting for his *maja*. He shuts
himself up in his room. Nobody comes. A whole day passes.
Two days pass. There's not a sign of life out of him, or on the
road. I start to worry. Is he dead? I ask myself as I go up to
his room. He's not dead but he wishes he were! I get him
something to eat and whilst he eats he tells me his story. In a
tavern near the Castellana he meets a young woman with
long black hair down to her waist and eyes like coals and they
dance all night. When it's time for her to go she says to him:
'Go on Thursday to Fuencarral. Near the wood you'll find an

inn. There you ask for the room which gives on to the
pomegranate tree and you wait for me there.'

GOYA: Did he tell you her name?

PEPA: I think he said Teresa.

GOYA: And afterwards? Did she come?

PEPA: No.

GARDENER: I can think of another Teresa who might well play
the same game. She too likes dressing up as a *maja* and
dancing in taverns. We've seen it with our own eyes, haven't
we?

GOYA: Shut your mouth.

PEPA: The poor boy waited a whole week. He couldn't believe she
wouldn't come. He made up excuse after excuse for her.

GARDENER: They all do.

PEPA: At the end my uncle asked him to pay and he didn't have
enough money. So he left his pistol as a forfeit. A beautiful
pistol, I can show it to you, made in Cordoba.

GARDENER: At least he didn't kill himself with it!

GOYA: Shut your mouth! A question, my girl, is the room always
called 'the room of the pomegranate tree'?

LEANDRO: (*Offstage*) Pepa!

(*Enter* LEANDRO *carrying loaves of bread, his apron covered
with flour.* PEPA *runs away from the table to join* LEANDRO.)

PEPA: Leandro! At last!

LEANDRO: I couldn't come yesterday. Had to help Father repair
the cart. (*He notices the mass of flowers.*) It's not true! Who's
died? I've never seen so many flowers.

PEPA: They're roses, Leandro. The stout gentleman brought
them. He has a rendezvous here. She hasn't come yet, he's
waiting for her.

GOYA: (*Shouting*) Listen, my girl, can you reply to my question?
When your young man asked for the room did he say: 'I want
the room with a window that looks out on to a pomegranate
tree?'

(PEPA *walks back to the table.*)

PEPA: Our third room it is, like I told you, always our favourite
. . . I don't understand what you're getting at, sir. Yes, he
said: 'Is there a room that looks out on to a pomegranate

41

tree?' But he was a poet. After he left when I was cleaning, I found some papers under his bed and on them were poems he'd begun to write.

GOYA: Poems!

PEPA: My uncle read one out loud. The poet compared her body to the stem of an autumn crocus, so fine it was, and so white.

GOYA: Crocus! And a brothel with a pomegranate tree! It was her! I can recognize her anywhere with my eyes shut. It was her! We're leaving. We're not waiting.

(*Exit* GOYA *and* GARDENER.)

LEANDRO: I want the truth, Pepa. Those flowers and that chest of frippery, he brought them for you. Otherwise he wouldn't leave them behind, would he? I arrive unexpectedly, so he beats a retreat.

PEPA: It's foolish to be so jealous, Leandro. They weren't for me. (*Unnoticed by the others, the* DUCHESS *arrives from behind the chapel. She is wearing a white dress, her hair down to her waist. She stares at the flowers. Leans against the wall, closes her eyes, immobile.*)

LEANDRO: You're hiding something from me.

PEPA: Nothing, my hawk, nothing. It's a story I don't understand either. Don't fret, my love. They live their lives their way. Kiss me instead.

(LEANDRO *and* PEPA *embrace. Lights fade.*)

ACT ONE

SCENE 6

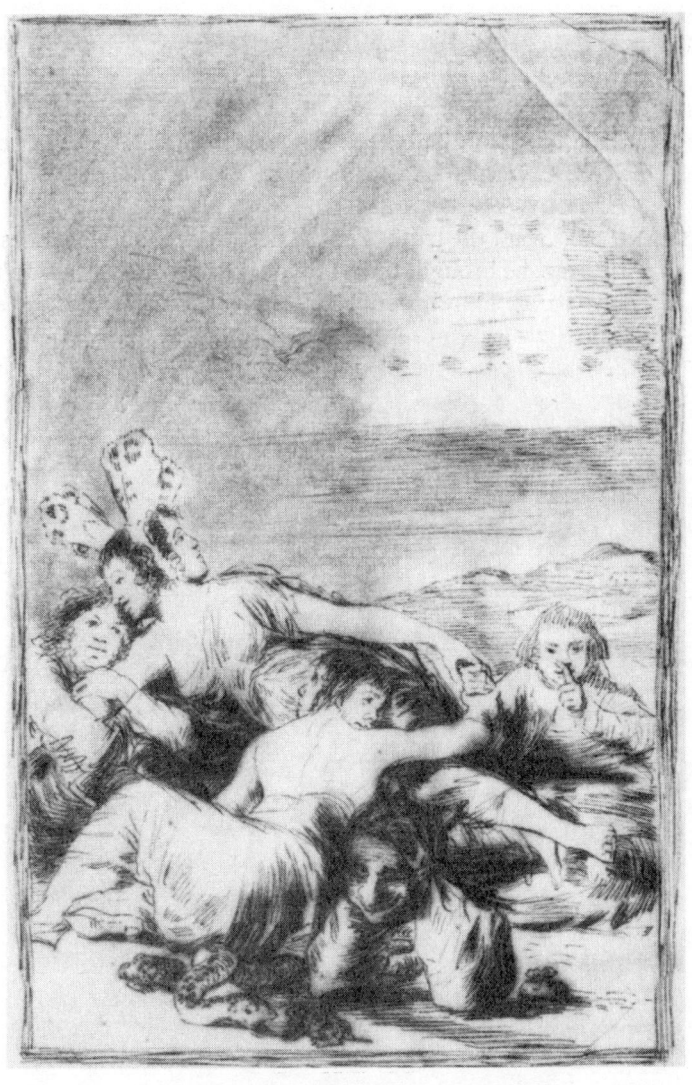

Sueño de la mentira
(drawing for Los Caprichos, The Prado, Madrid)

Autumn afternoon (1794). Garden of Duchess's residence. (There is no carriage.) A very low hammock hangs where, in scene 4, the child's bed stood. In it reclines DUCHESS. GOYA *lies on ground beside her, gently swinging hammock.* DUCHESS *is singing a kind of lullaby.*

DUCHESS: Seigneur saves his honour
                    Rides away proud.
                The mad in the tower
                Are laughing out loud.
GOYA: What do we do when we're alone together?
DUCHESS: Everyone knows. It's proverbial.
GOYA: Say it. I want to hear your voice saying the words.
DUCHESS: Saying what everyone knows –
GOYA: Everyone is wrong. For we are never alone together!
    That's the truth. A month in the country. Those were your
    words, and in no time you forget! Take me to Fuencarral –
    I've never been there . . . Those were your words – words out
    of your own mouth.
DUCHESS: I fancy, inquisitor, the interrogation should now come
    to an end.
    (*Sings:*) The mad in their tower
        Are laughing out loud.
GOYA: What you offer, you take away.
DUCHESS: Then take all.
GOYA: In your lying hammock there's only place for one.
DUCHESS: Upset me then! Capsize your duchess. And we'll make
    love come down . . .
    (*Enter* WIDOW *dressed as dueña of Duchess's household.*)
    . . . down among the tombs! Capsize me!
WIDOW: A day of omens, Doña Cayetana, a day of undeniable
    omens. Last night the full moon, and not any one as you
    might imagine, but the hunter's full moon, as pregnant as
    our cook Lola. At dawn you woke up with both sheets fallen
    down on the Toledo tiles, even the one you were lying on. At

midday a swarm of bees in the plum tree. And now who should come but Don Antonio!

DUCHESS: You confuse everything. Don Antonio's coming is always good news.

WIDOW: More, he has not come empty-handed, and what he has brought to show us is something neither your eyes nor mine have ever looked upon.

GOYA: (*To* DUCHESS) Get rid of her!

DUCHESS: I want to look at what Don Antonio has brought for me.

(WIDOW *beckons* TONIO *who enters holding his hands over his shirt.* DWARF *and* DOCTOR *follow. Distant sound of music. Everyone gathers round* TONIO *to look at what he is carrying in his shirt.*)

TONIO: I found her in the Guadarrama a month ago. She's almost tame now.

DWARF: Pity the rabbits! She hypnotizes them with her gaze. And eats them for dinner.

TONIO: Didn't Raphael paint one, Francisco?

GOYA: Raphael was a fornicator.

DWARF: In the winter she wears white. Except for the tip of her tail which is black.

DUCHESS: Her coat is softer than a baby's hair.

GOYA: It was Leonardo. Except it wasn't a little brute like this, it was an ermine.

DUCHESS: How did you capture her?

DWARF: (*Singing*) Elle court, elle court, messieurs
        Elle est passée par ici
        Elle repassera par là.

TONIO: I found her on the grass by the edge of the Madrid – Salamanca autoroute.

DOCTOR: The ancient Greek name for the species is *Galata*. Which today is also the name of a district in Istanbul.

GOYA: They talk, they talk . . .

DUCHESS: Look at her eyes!

DWARF: Elle court, elle court, messieurs!

DUCHESS: Look at her eyes. Nothing deceives her. She knows what she wants. Why don't you call her Cayetana?

TONIO: Cayetana it is!

DUCHESS: Will the name Cayetana put a rabbit to sleep?

(DUCHESS *approaches* DWARF, *who pretends to fall asleep.*)

WIDOW: Do you know what the midwives say? They say this creature conceives by way of the ear and gives birth by way of the mouth.

GOYA: Everything said in this bog is mad. It begins in the house and it goes on in the garden.

DUCHESS: To conceive by the ear! There's an idea of genius. Pure genius.

DOCTOR: Here we should note, my dear, the constant ambiguity which touches everything concerning the ear as a symbolic organ: an organ which lends itself to both sensual and spiritual raptures. The male word enters the ear just as sperm enters the vagina to make its spiral way to the uterus and there to fertilize the ovule. Seminal fluid and Divine Words are interchangeable. The Annunciation is a perfect example of this ambivalence.

DUCHESS: What a mind you have, Doctor! Your ideas show us how to fly! Poets, philosophers, musicians all conceiving in the way you describe. You've turned my head. Engender, engender! Play for me.

(*Music begins. Suddenly* GOYA *charges the dancers and one by one, chases them offstage.*)

GOYA: Out, black! Out, seersucker! Out, little cleavage! Out, hosiery! Out, blood! I'll thrash you like wheat!

(EXIT *all except* DUCHESS.)

So quickly fled! Alone with my own voice now. Silence. Come brother voice and show your mettle. Cayetana! Cayetana, who gives birth and kills through her teeth! Cayetana the witch!

DUCHESS: How dare you! Those people belong to my household. Go back to where you came from, go home to your twenty children you spawn like a frog – go back to your long-suffering wife.

GOYA: When you look in the mirror, do you see your lies? Do you tie them under your chin and press them against your eyes so you can't hear the truth?

DUCHESS: Shouting can't frighten me. Do you really believe, you little mule from Aragon, that I've inherited none of the courage of my forebears? Do you think you can shout words at me like you throw stones at a bitch in your backyard?

GOYA: Easier to cover her nakedness with a scrap of flannelette than to hide her lies. Her lies are too long to cover . . . too sinuous. And they bleed too much, they leave stains on the Toledo tiles.

(*Re-enter* DOCTOR, *unnoticed by others.*)

DUCHESS: Silence!

GOYA: We, who are born in the dust, know better how to lie. We make good liars. We also know how to boast. This baturro standing here, was born a goatherd. He painted the finest cupola in Saragossa. He was appointed Artist of the King's Household. He decorated outrageously the church of San Antonio de la Florida. And he lays the Thirteenth Duchess of Alba!

DUCHESS: You mix the gossip of washerwomen with the vanity of a peacock.

GOYA: Paint me in black, she says. I don't paint in black, lady, I paint in muck. I paint you all in muck – with your ribbons and lace and organdie and gold. You marvel and you thank me, because you think, with my slime and my smearing, I've confessed you! The priests listen to your sins and give you absolution. I listen to what you look like, and you go away, all of you, believing your appearances have been forgiven.

DUCHESS: Turn your back. Your jealousy is too ugly.

DOCTOR: He's demented.

DUCHESS: Nobody on this earth has the right to tell me how to treat my guests, or how to spend my time. If I choose to dance, Frogman, I will dance, alone or in company, with or without music. You paint in shit, you confess us and what do you understand? Nothing. Don't you realize there are not many afternoons for dancing left? Don't you know there are no more nights than there are afternoons? Except the last one, Paco, the night which puts an end to all afternoons!

GOYA: She flies by night and she lays her breasts on the hands of the first comer.

48

DOCTOR: A brainstorm's burning out the cochlea nerve!

DUCHESS: What do you want with our two lives? Answer me! It's an order. Our so poor mortality. What do you want, Paco? Tell me and I'll listen.

GOYA: (*Taking his head between his hands*) In this boulder there's so much water, strike it, strike it like Abraham struck the rock! There's enough water between these ears, Cayetana, to quench the thirst of all your Father's horses. Strike it!

DUCHESS: Come. We'll whisper to each other. Quietly. Alone. (*To* DOCTOR) I want you to leave us alone. I want to be alone with my bull.

DOCTOR: (*Leaving*) Auditory perception now nil.

DUCHESS: (*Leading* GOYA *to hammock*) Just the two of us. I'll tell you what's never been told, what I've never even told to myself. When the Duke of Alba plays his everlasting music, I dream. And what do I dream of? I dream of you when you are roused, when you are man as I've never known man before. I want to be nothing but your covering. Throw me your dust. You who are man as Cayetana will never know another. What will you throw at me, my love? A knife here (*Her heart*)? It is yours already. A river to drown in? I am drowned. What will you throw at me? Throw me your dust, my bull. Say something. Say my name. Scream it if you want. Name me another name then . . . What do you want to call me?

GOYA: I can't hear you!

DUCHESS: Scream it if you want to!

GOYA: What are you saying?

DUCHESS: My love, my love! Anything!

GOYA: So quickly fled – all, all to the last word.

DUCHESS: Speak to me! (*She shouts louder and louder.*)
Paco! Paco! Paco! (*Duchess throws herself on her knees, clutching at the hammock which swings. Goya stands immobile.*)
     The mad in their tower
     Are laughing out loud!
(*Enter* DWARF.)

DUCHESS: He can hear nothing, nothing, *nada*. I've made him go deaf.

We must never leave him, never . . . Promise me, Amore?
(*Sound of jet fighter. Lights fade.*)

ACT TWO

SCENE I

The dog
(The Prado, Madrid)

Front of stage before semi-transparent curtain – through which is visible cemetery transformed into a landscape of boulders. Enter DWARF, *still dressed as in Act One, rolling a white carriage wheel as a hoop.*

DWARF: I told you we might all die of laughter – anyway we are dying. The Duchess of Alba died of food poisoning. Our country made war on France to save the principle of monarchy. There are flies everywhere this summer. We made peace with France to save ourselves. Then the *gavachos* kidnapped the He-Goat, the Whore and the Blood Sausage and are keeping them as hostages in Bayonne. More flies, more vultures than anybody can remember. Napoleon sat his brother Joseph on our throne and sent in his army to liberate us, to help us throw off the shackles of the past. His soldiers threw our women on their backs. Some are collaborating with the French to the death so Spain can become a modern country – with fewer rags and fewer uniforms. Some are fighting the French to the death, because they'll give their lives to keep Spain as it is. 'Who liberates who from what?' is one of history's worst jokes. The Year of the Blind, it's called, the Year of Our Lord, 1808. There's very little to eat. The rich still have their hair done. It's stifling hot. I've kept my promise to the Duchess and I've stayed with her painter. We're going to Aragon.

(DWARF *swats fly and rolls his hoop offstage. Transparent curtain rises to disclose landscape of boulders. The colour of rust. Enter* GOYA *and* DWARF *in dark tattered clothes.* GOYA *is now aged sixty. When he speaks, the* DWARF *has often to shout or repeat his words, for his companion is deaf.*)

GOYA: (*Pointing*) At the foot of that rock, there's a dog howling.

DWARF: Let's both sit on it. We need a rest.

(*They sit.*)

GOYA: Look between my legs! There's a town there. Where your foot's dangling, the dog's howling.

DWARF: If you say so. What town is it, Don Francisco? WHAT TOWN?

GOYA: Saragossa.

DWARF: The town we're going to?

GOYA: All rocks are prophetic. What can you see, Amore?

DWARF: Figures running away in panic. What fire leaves behind. Smoke. A man on his knees, face upturned towards us, face that his mother put against her breast, cut like meat into suffering. If I was a man, I'd kill him out of pity. Behind him, a gulley, with corpses, some with French boots, some with shoes made of serge . . . Who built this town? WHO IS THERE?

GOYA: The giants. How do you know, Amore, you're not imagining everything you're telling me?

DWARF: I can't be. I have a cheerful imagination. As soon as I imagine, it's a joke! Do you like chicken? If it's cooked, yes. Do you like mule? If it's smoked, yes. Do you like fish? If it's dried, yes. Do you like milk? If she unbuttons her blouse, please! I never imagine anything as bad as life.

GOYA: I have no imagination. None at all.

DWARF: They say you are a visionary.

GOYA: I put down what I see.

DWARF: I've heard it said that in what you put down you exaggerate!

GOYA: What?

DWARF: EXAGGERATE.

GOYA: Blind fools! Appearances tell all. There's nothing they can't tell. Fools! There's no exaggeration that goes further than them. God, Amore, has left us alone with the visible, like deserting us in hell. He, the seer, is invisible. We with our flesh and hair, mucus and bones, are condemned to be seen. And worse than that, we are condemned to face what we see.

DWARF: Why don't you shut your eyes?

GOYA: When somebody's dead, you can see it from two hundred yards away, their silhouette goes cold.

DWARF: Let's think about the chicken all golden in the oven.

GOYA: It's full of fossils, that rock. If I say it is bleeding, do I
    exaggerate?
DWARF: (*Nodding*) You do.
GOYA: Correct. If I say we can shelter behind it, am I
    exaggerating?
DWARF: (*Shaking his head*) No.
GOYA: There are men whose faces are the most indecent parts of
    their whole bodies, and it would be a good thing if they put
    their faces in their breeches.
DWARF: Have you seen these men?
GOYA: I can't hear you. You shout, you make faces and I can't
    hear you! In Saragossa God is going to leave us.
    (*Sound of jet fighter. Lights dim.*)

ACT TWO

SCENE 2

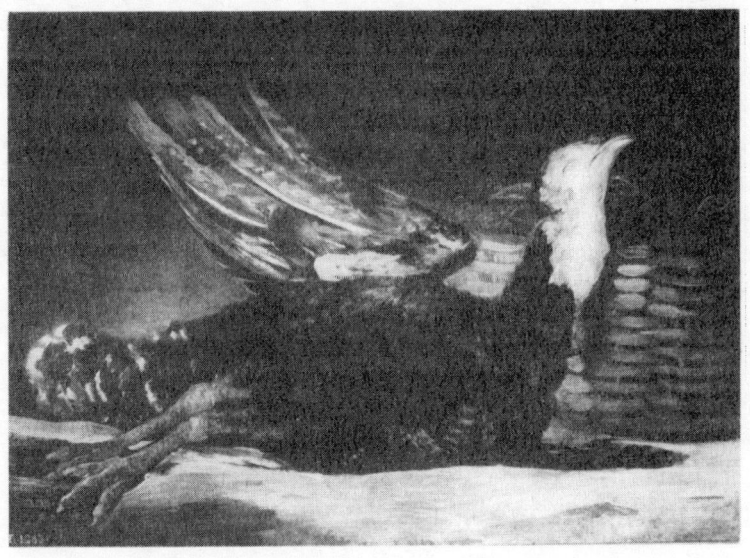

Dead bird
(The Prado, Madrid)

Cemetery transformed into ruins of Saragossa. August 1808. The
deserted chapel is a ruined room in the city under siege. There are sacks
of wool, sandbags. GOYA *is seated at a table, looking at a sketchbook.*
From time to time there is the smoke and dust of explosions, distant
and near. The silence is total.

GOYA: (*To audience*) You can't hear anything, can you? You're
 like me. You've switched off the sound. The image is grainy,
 but it's live. Did you see the wall of the house back there
 disintegrating slowly without a sound? Sickeningly slowly.
 Falling. Did you see the people being buried underneath the
 rubble without a scream? No sound. Bombardments don't
 stop at night, and it's not yet night.
 (GOYA *looks through broken window on to cemetery. Enter*
 DWARF, *dressed in tattered, dust-covered uniform.*)
 Amore's back. Up to God knows what.
 (DWARF *climbs on to a pile of rubble and pretends to read a*
 proclamation.)
DWARF: Heroic people of Saragossa, city of two cathedrals, take
 heed and listen, for it is your very own General Don José
 Palafox who speaks to you.
 (*Noise like a loudspeaker being adjusted.*)
 Women of Saragossa, you who have shown yourselves
 willing to sacrifice body and soul for the defence of our city,
 you whose fighting example has been an inspiration to every
 one of us, pick up now your spades and your shovels and
 your brooms, clear the streets, fill the sandbags, fortify our
 city. The French army will die of mortification knowing it
 has been vanquished by you; our mothers, our sisters, our
 wives, our fiancées. I am your father, women of Saragossa!
 (*Aside*) He's just turned twenty-eight our young Palafox . . . I
 am your father! Death to the Invader!
 (*Exit* DWARF.)
GOYA: During bombardments as many die in the dark as in the

light, perhaps more, because rescue work is harder – unless enough fires have been started, and the fires turn night into day. (*He turns a page of the sketchbook on the table.*) Palafox is a fool. Don José Palafox. No brains. I've studied him. Look at his mug. It's the face of a handsome bison. He looks better when mounted . . . which is why Her Highness the Whore gave him the second command of her Palace Guard. (*He closes book.*) One fire leads to another. I see a firestorm silently devouring a whole city in one night – flames, wind, a pillar of smoke, no explosion. Only ashes. The city is on a river like this one. The river Ebre and the river Elbe. I see an unborn soldier, who is not yet a foetus, lecturing on the military use of firestorms. His listeners are moths. Shh! I can hear their wings.

(*Enter* TONIO, *fifty, dressed like an irregular soldier, walking with great difficulty, one leg wrapped in dirty cloth. He embraces* GOYA.)

TONIO: At last you're here. I never doubted for an instant you'd come in the end.

GOYA: By mule Fuendetodos is half a day's journey. I was born in Fuendetodos. I've come to see my mother.

TONIO: I thought your mother was dead.

GOYA: A mere detail – what's happened to your leg?

TONIO: Masonry from a wall fell on my foot. You could see nothing for dust. I felt nothing at the time. We were charging a cannon under heavy mortar fire. We protect our heads with wool sacks. (*Smiling,* TONIO *picks up a sack and places it on his head.*) The whole world is watching us. The victors of Marengo and Austerlitz and Ulm shall not pass! The most powerful military machine in the world cannot quench our resistance. And why? Because they are lost. They have only maps. And the ruins are still our home. Have you seen our women? What have you seen?

GOYA: Was it a twenty-four-pound cannon?

TONIO: (*Nodding*) Yes.

GOYA: With iron wheels?

TONIO: Yes. Agostina – like a flower of flame. She seized a fuse from the hands of a dying artilleryman and fired a round of canister point-blank at the *gavachos*. They fell back. They couldn't advance.

GOYA: I can see you're feverish, Tonio. Come and sit. How much longer can you hold out?

TONIO: Only you could ask such a question. It's like asking God: How long will I live?

GOYA: How long?

(TONIO *makes the sign of 50 with his fingers*.)

Fifty! Fifty hours?

TONIO: Not hours! Weeks. I'm a member of the Junta. With Tio Jorge, the water carrier, with Dom Basilio Bogueiro de Santiago, scholar and strategist, with Pedro . . . How did you get here? It's a miracle. God himself must have brought you.

GOYA: Who?

TONIO: GOD.

GOYA: Do you think God comes to places like this?

TONIO: God's love is so large it seems indifference. You shouldn't go out when they are shelling.

(*Dust and smoke. No sound.*)

GOYA: The giants protect me.

TONIO: There are drawings in your notebook?

GOYA: The giants have no memory.

TONIO: When they bombarded the hospital, it was she who organized the evacuation of the sick.

GOYA: Who did you say?

TONIO: The Countess Burita. She has a strange power. I was there when the asylum was bombed. I saw what she could do with the mad. THE MAD.

GOYA: The mad are innocent – even the raving ones they shut in cages suspended from the ceiling, even they are innocent. The truly rabidly mad are not shut up. Never. They are out there at liberty – pursuing their madness. Every century, pursuing it.

TONIO: She saved their lives.

GOYA: There was an innocent madman praying at the foot of the Cross in the Coso. He said he was the river Ebre and he was going to extinguish, with his waters, every fire in the city.

TONIO: It's six years since she died, isn't it?

61

GOYA: I saw another one wearing a loincloth – he was walking where the shells were falling like rain, and he was eating his own fingers.

TONIO: It's six years since Cayetana died, isn't it?

GOYA: Tonio, don't shout, please don't shout each time you mention her name.

(*An inaudible explosion very near the room. Dust falls everywhere.*)

Who is nursing who?

TONIO: I'm talking of the wounded nursed by the Countess Burita.

GOYA: Don't shout when you mention her name!

TONIO: Not Cayetana.

GOYA: You hold your head like a man who believes in God. Not like me. It's a question of the chin. He holds it up for you.

TONIO: She's twenty-two. Her hair would come down to her feet, I think.

GOYA: At dawn her body weighed nothing.

TONIO: Her?

GOYA: Cayetana's.

TONIO: Desire is cruel, desire is like hope. It summons you by name. And there's nothing can quench it.

GOYA: Why doesn't she nurse you?

TONIO: With me you can never get rid of hope. Trying to get rid of hope is a lost cause with me.

(*Enter* DWARF *to proclaim on pile of rubble.*)

DWARF: Heroic people of Saragossa, city of two cathedrals, take heed and listen, for it is your very own General Don José Palafox who speaks to you. At this hour I'm not asking you for courage. You have proved you have enough, and to spare. You have listened to me and redoubled your efforts to implement the fortifications of the city. I am speaking now to warn you that the evil, which comes from the Devil's side of the Pyrenees, does not only take the form of cannon balls and shrapnel, musket fire and sabres. This same evil can insidiously enter your mind and the minds of your neighbours. Everywhere in our city Treason is today waiting for its chance. There are traitors among you. Be vigilant,

people of Saragossa. Banish the enemy within! Denounce
those who, disguised beneath cloaks like your own, harbour
poisonous thoughts against King and Country. Denounce
the spies! Denounce the traitors! Denounce the heretics!

TONIO: The French sent us an ultimatum an hour ago. It was
three words long. *Peace and Capitulation.*

(DWARF *comes into ruined room.*)

DWARF: In the New Market there's not a scrap of food of any sort
for sale, only men hung from gibbets. Spaniards hung by
Spaniards. Under the arches a few crouch over fires cooking
something. (*Hands bread to* GOYA.) It's for you, Don
Francisco, a present from a phantom under the arcades.

GOYA: The reply?

TONIO: War to the death, guerra a cuchillo.

(GOYA *takes out a packet, wrapped in cloth, from under his shirt
and throws it on the table.*)

Drawings?

GOYA: No. Money. Money for the defence of Saragossa.

TONIO: My friend!

GOYA: I've been well paid by the French.

TONIO: WHAT?

GOYA: Arts, crafts, services.

(TONIO *tries to embrace* GOYA, *who seizes* TONIO's *sabre and
makes to attack his own cape, hung on a nail.*)

Give a cape to a thief and it will hide his loot. Give a cape to
an informer and he will pass unnoticed. Give the power of
the cape to a caudillo or a Führer or a madman in the
Pentagon and he'll liquidate, burn alive, make bombs in the
form of toys. Slash the capes! Slash the shirt beneath! Slash
the flesh! Slash the guts! Slash the heart! What do you see?
Darkness. Nothingness. Blackness. Blackness, Tonio, only
blackness.

TONIO: No. Francisco, no. We never die. Saragossa will triumph.
Nothing on earth can put an end to us.

GOYA: You forget one thing.

TONIO: Tell me.

GOYA: You forget fatigue. It's like rust, fatigue. It eats into the
strongest wills, saps the noblest energies, turns into red dust

the most fervent hopes. Finally, fatigue chooses the easy
solution, the shortest answer, whatever is at hand. It doesn't
happen immediately, it takes its time, but before the end,
fatigue, the exterminating angel of fatigue, takes over.

TONIO: Saragossa is resisting. This is the truth before our very
eyes. And the same truth is here – in our hearts.

GOYA: You can hardly stand on your feet.

TONIO: So long as Saragossa withstands, she resists for everyone
now and in the times to come. Saragossa salutes Stalingrad!
And you, Francisco, you're our pledge, a pledge that what
we're living will never be forgotten. Promise me, Francisco,
PROMISE ME!

GOYA: You believe in promises, my poor Tonio, at a moment like
this!

TONIO: It's not true you have no more faith, Francisco, I don't
believe it. You are faith itself. Faith can't leave you. (*He gets
to his feet with difficulty.*) They need me out there. (*He picks
up packet of money.*) We'll buy saltpetre, bandages,
medicines, gunpowder.

GOYA: Each step you take hurts you.

TONIO: That you should have come, it's a miracle. Watch us,
Francisco. The corpses between sandbags. The cruelty.
Watch us. Every birth and every ruin is a window that gives
on to God. Remind him of our glory!

(Exit TONIO. GOYA *puts cloak on his shoulders, comes to the
table, takes notebook. For the first time the deafening noise of
bombardment. Lights fade.*)

SCENE 3

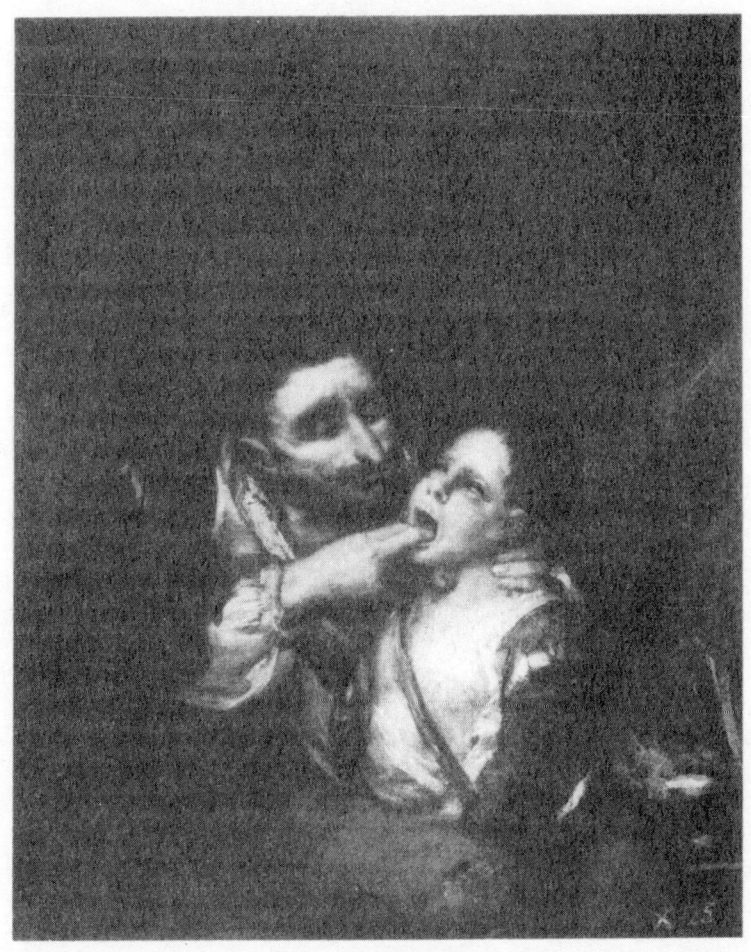

Lazarillo de Tormes
(Private collection, Madrid)

End of winter afternoon. Widow as GOYA'S MOTHER *in her kitchen.*
(By entrance to chapel.) She is seated at a table, peeling potatoes.
Enter GOYA, *exactly as seen in previous scene.*

MOTHER: I met the curé this afternoon. He's pleased with you.
　　He says you draw well. Nobody in Fuendetodos has ever
　　seen such beautiful drawings. Say your prayers and eat your
　　muffin, I've kept it warm for you. Take your time, don't be
　　in such a rush, you'll burn your tongue. You rush at
　　everything. You eat too fast, it's gone before you can say
　　Jack Knife. You pray too fast. Do you hear me, Chico?
GOYA: I can hear you, Mother.
MOTHER: They say you're making a lot of money at school, is that
　　true?
GOYA: Five hundred reales per head painted. It varies according
　　to the sitter. Sometimes a thousand.
MOTHER: Be thrifty, Chico. The smarter the clothes, the dirtier
　　the mud that sticks. Be thrifty with yourself and your
　　earnings. Have you thought of what you'll leave behind?
GOYA: It's being prepared.
MOTHER: That's good. Take your time.
GOYA: I have some money for you.
MOTHER: Keep it, I don't need anything now. Ghosts have no
　　needs – it's a strange advantage. At nine months you were
　　already walking. You stood on a stool to look out of the
　　window. I was still nursing you at the breast. And at ten
　　months you were running.
GOYA: I think I'm ill, Mother.
MOTHER: None of us has ever died of deafness. If you don't hear,
　　you have to look harder.
GOYA: My head goes round and round and there's a ringing like a
　　bell. Things scratch and boom and fly in my head. Djinns
　　and gnomes and vampires, bats and suckers and tell-tales
　　with eyes of owls and cats' paws. Am I mad, Mother?

MOTHER: At school you'd do better to listen to your teacher. Eat
your muffin and spread the butter on it. Shh! Your father's
come back from Saragossa on the mule. These days he earns
five reales a week, gilding frames. Now wash your hands,
Chico . . . The gold leaf sticks to his thumbs and frightens
the birds. Do what I say, Chico sweetie, only onions make
you cry. Don't ever forget the candles for the Nuestra Señora
del Pilar. When you're a man, you'll be happy, don't forget.
Does your wife Josefa take good care of you in school?
GOYA: She is so light, Mama. She's scarcely there. She can do
nothing for me.
MOTHER: She can do nothing, she can do nothing – how could she
do anything for you? Even her offspring don't live more than
a few days. People say she smothers them.
GOYA: The children, my children – they're my fault, Mama.
MOTHER: There's no love in her heart. That's the beginning and
end of it. Neither for you nor for the children.
GOYA: It's my fault.
MOTHER: Women are cruel, Chico, many are witches. They
dream only of sucking you dry, blood and brains.
GOYA: Their breasts are so soft to touch, their skin so white and
their eyes like coals to warm you.
MOTHER: You see, Chico, it's better now. Everything's better.
Have a little sleep. It's a long way to Madrid from
Fuendetodos.
(*Darkness.*)

ACT TWO

SCENE 4

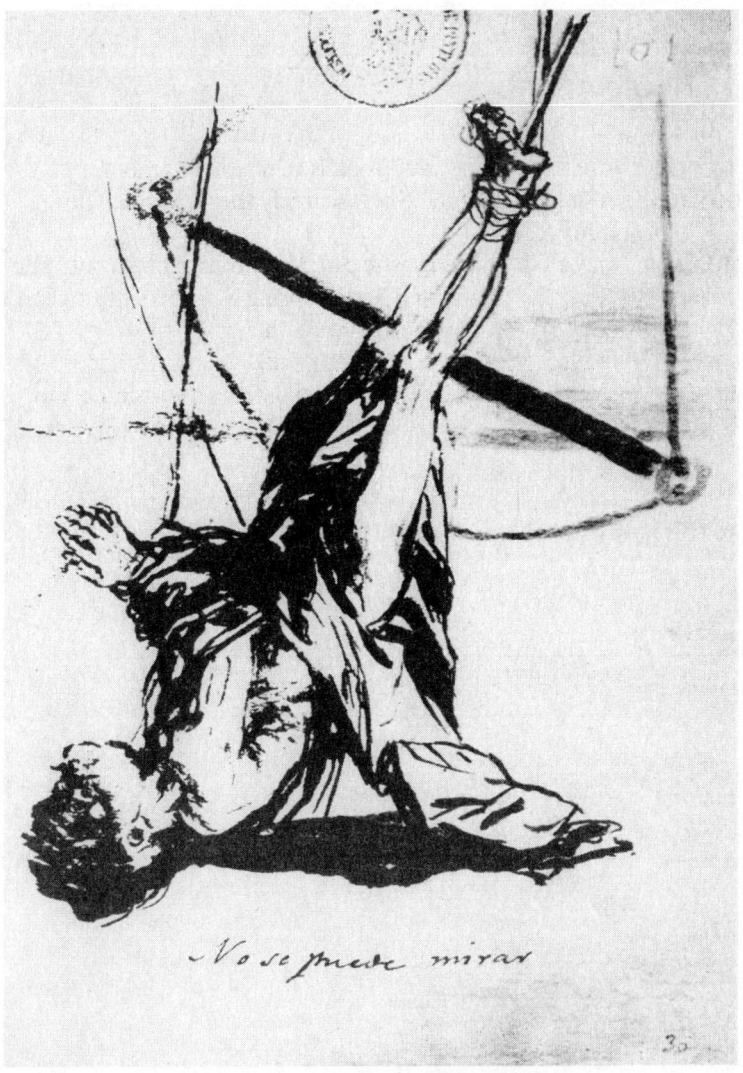

No se puede mirar
(drawing for Los Caprichos, The Prado, Madrid)

Day. Aragon (1809). GOYA, *led by* DWARF, *is crossing an arid landscape of boulders, made in the cemetery. The colour of rust.*

GOYA: We are being watched all the while.

DWARF: On this stage of rocks I can't see a soul. Not a horse, not even a mule, has passed along this road since midday.

GOYA: If you want to speak to me, you'd better climb on to a rock, I can't keep bending down all the time.

DWARF: In which case should we carry a rock with us? CARRY IT?

GOYA: Why not? You can carry it, and it'll serve us as a permanent hiding place.

DWARF: The only problem is one of choice. How to choose one rock from so many?

GOYA: Ours is a country of broken mountains.
(They stop. DWARF *picks up rock.)*

DWARF: I try to imagine that instead of my carrying this rock, it's you.

GOYA: If only we could exchange! You take my load, I'll carry your rock!

DWARF: *(Cunningly)* It wouldn't work. Like that I wouldn't have anything to stand on, and you wouldn't hear me.
(They walk on. DWARF *stands on rock.)*
Do you think there's an end?

GOYA: To what?

DWARF: This.

GOYA: No.

DWARF: Saragossa fell.

GOYA: With those who fought there.

DWARF: Fifty thousand souls departed.
(They walk on.)

GOYA: The sight of agony is more terrible than the sight of death.

DWARF: I'm going to put the rock down here because I think we should hide behind it immediately.
(They hide behind rock.)

71

GOYA: Tonio is dead. I can see his corpse, stiff.

DWARF: Better think of his glory in the everlasting annals of Saragossa.

GOYA: What do you hear?

DWARF: Nothing. Nothing at all. Not a horse, not a mule, not a soul on the steppe. The rock was too heavy, that's all . . . I wish we were in Madrid. They have fireworks every night to celebrate the Saint Napoleon! Imagine the rockets above the Puerta del Sol! The sparks falling like confetti. Our Joseph has abolished all feudal duties to the Señores. We're becoming the Promised Land.

GOYA: Let's get to our feet and continue.

DWARF: Do you hear the vultures?

GOYA: I can't hear. Do you want me to repeat it?

DWARF: Perhaps they heard the news from Madrid. Perhaps that's why they're squalling.

GOYA: Fewer cloaks, fewer cloaks! Fewer cloaks! That's what they cry. Lift it up again.

DWARF: No question, this steppe has a soul. Look at it! *Nada*. An army can cross it and it's like a ship at sea, it makes a wake.

GOYA: Lift it up again.

DWARF: Then in no time it disappears without a trace, without a single trace.

GOYA: I'm going to sit on it whilst you carry it.

DWARF: I'm not strong enough.

GOYA: You underestimate your powers. There's already a town on your rock.

DWARF: I'm going to put the rock down because I think we should hide behind it immediately.

GOYA: You said that before. It turned out to be laziness.
    (*They hide behind the rock.*)

DWARF: Cover your face, hide your papers and look hungry!
    (*Enter* LEANDRO *dressed as a bandit with pistol. He kicks at the two lying figures.*)

LEANDRO: On your feet, both! Hands up high.

DWARF: If we had any arms, we'd have sold them long ago in the hope of acquiring a bite to eat.

LEANDRO: Money? Gold? Jewellery?

DWARF: Young man, what do you expect? You must be new at the game. This is the eleventh time we've been robbed! (*Glances at* GOYA.) No, I won't exaggerate. It's the third. We have nothing left. Search us.

LEANDRO: Where are you making for?

DWARF: He's deaf, he can't hear. I have to step on the rock there to make him hear.

LEANDRO: What's his business?

DWARF: Poultry.

LEANDRO: Where have you come from?

DWARF: Chickens, geese, duck, pheasants, guinea fowl, quail, hoopoes, linnets, nightingales.

LEANDRO: Open his cloak.

DWARF: Not a feather now. He lost them all. That's why we had to leave.

LEANDRO: Did the French pillage you?

DWARF: (*Hedging*) A bit of French, yes, these days you can never be sure. A bit of wolves too. Every feather gone.

LEANDRO: I'm taking you back to the camp. The Tinker has to question you.

DWARF: The Tinker?

LEANDRO: Before he took to the mountains, he ground knives in the villages.

DWARF: There's no point in questioning him (*He nods at* GOYA.) He can't hear.

LEANDRO: Did you pass any troops?

DWARF: I'll ask him . . . No, he says, it wasn't a wolf, it was a fox. He hasn't seen any French since he sold them his last goose. This goose was a favourite of his and when he had to part with her, he had tears in his eyes.

LEANDRO: Don't fuck around with me.

DWARF: He understands nothing about what's going on. He can't hear. He doesn't know the difference between a tortilla and an omelette. You haven't by any chance got anything to eat? It's been days.

LEANDRO: On your feet! I'm taking you to the Tinker.

DWARF: It's a fine flask you've got there, *guerrillero*, I wonder what's in it – water?

LEANDRO: You covet what's in the bottle, dwarf?

DWARF: For us it has a medical use. A few drops in each ear and the hearing comes back a little.

(LEANDRO, *gun pointed, starts to walk the two men off*.)

LEANDRO: I warn you. We are learning to count in the mountains now. For one Spaniard dead, we kill four prisoners. And we don't waste precious shot and powder on them. We chase the *gavachos* and their friends over the cliff.

DWARF: That's justice, *guerrilleros*!

LEANDRO: The *gavachos* raped two nuns in Asasua and cut off their heads. The *gavachos* took two of our wounded and impaled them on the branches of a fruit tree. Two and two make four, so the Tinker counted sixteen. Sixteen at the foot of the precipice there.

GOYA: And so it goes.

LEANDRO: What did the old man say?

DWARF: He says you'll fight till the last *gavacho* is kicked back over the Pyrenees. He says there's no other people on earth who defend their country – like we Spaniards defend our Spain.

(*Exit* LEANDRO *with his two prisoners. Sudden darkness.*)

ACT TWO

SCENE 5

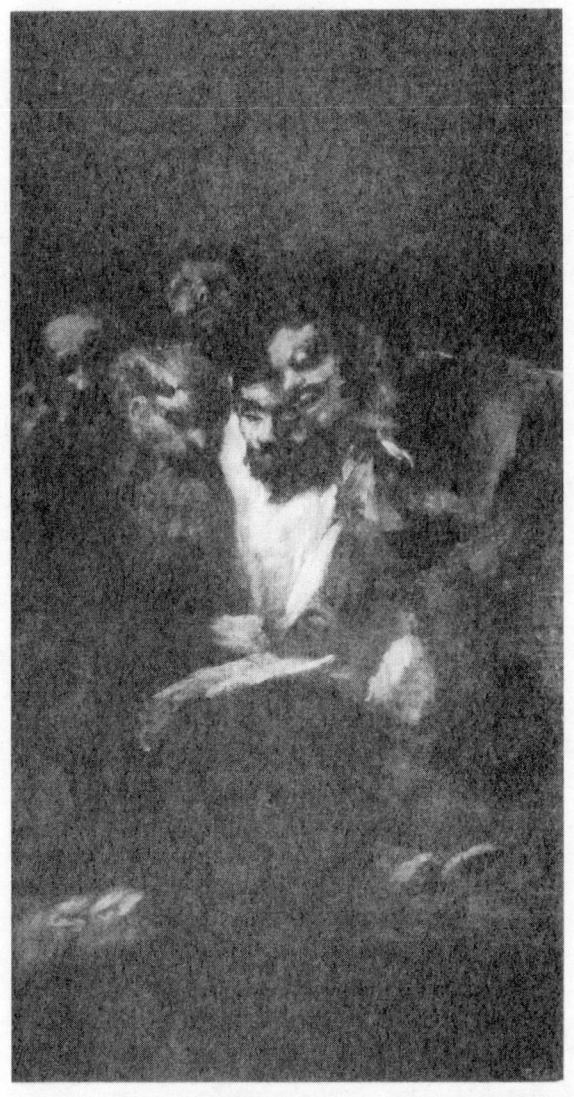

Hommes lisant
(The Prado, Madrid)

Evening (1809). Two chairs and a table with many papers on it, set back before a semi-transparent curtain. Behind the curtain a firework display. FEDERICO, *seated at the table, is watching the display.*

FEDERICO: 'Let Socialism be
                      in the teeth of all conflicts
                      for us a monument struck
                      in common bronze.'*

(*Enter* DOCTOR *hurriedly.*)

DOCTOR: Calls everywhere. Rushed off my feet, my friend. All the French with stomach complaints. But you – I must say you look in very good shape. Fine fettle.

(FEDERICO *offers* DOCTOR *a glass.*)

A strange phenomenon and it's not the first time I've noticed it. Men come out of prison either broken or with more energy than before. And that's your case, if I may say so, Don Federico. I wonder at times if I shouldn't prescribe a mild dose of incarceration as a cure for lassitude, ennui, disinterest. That makes you smile?

FEDERICO: The only thing to be said for a cell, Doctor, is that you can learn in it a certain detachment from the present and a certain receptiveness, I'd almost say tenderness, towards the future.

DOCTOR: The future?

FEDERICO: Tell me, do you believe there's such a thing as progress in the science of medicine?

DOCTOR: Undoubtedly. Though the idea of progress doesn't suppress pain as effectively as morphine.

(*Behind the screen the flaring of fireworks in the sky.*)

Look! Fireworks. And not, for once, cannon fire!

FEDERICO: They were already dancing in the park when I came home.

*From a late poem by Mayakovsky.

DOCTOR: (*Touching papers on table*) A new publication? May I ask what it's about? Your imagination in full flight?

FEDERICO: It's a translation.

DOCTOR: From what foreign language?

FEDERICO: Not exactly from a foreign language. Rather it's a rendering into the language of today the experience of the future.

DOCTOR: Ah! That's unexpected. I've recognized for a long time the gifts of your intelligence and your reasoning, but I was altogether ignorant of your gift of prophecy. May I?

(FEDERICO *nods*, DOCTOR *takes the top page, reads:*)

    'Let Socialism be
      in the teeth of all conflicts
      for us a monument struck
      in common bronze.'

Socialism? The word must come from the Latin *socius*, no? Something to do with word *society*; or the word *social*, I suppose. What do you understand by it? Socialism?

FEDERICO: It is what I'm working on whenever I have a minute. More or less it refers to the organization of a social body for the benefit of the common good rather than private interest. Based on a principle which is the opposite of egoism.

DOCTOR: Not so fast . . . not so quick. A social body? I have enough trouble with each individual human body. Can you think of society as being like a body? Above all, can you construct a society, a body, as you deem fit?

FEDERICO: That is our task. It will take a long time.

DOCTOR: Are you sure you will not find yourself in opposition to what is natural and perhaps changeless? Let me give an example from the human body. The heart. Blood flows from the heart by the left ventricle and returns through the veins to the right ventricle. Is it possible to imagine this flow being reversed? The blood leaving the heart at the right and entering at the left?

FEDERICO: Surely not. But with a social body anything is possible. It is man's creation.

DOCTOR: There's a suspicious whiff of poetry in what you are proposing.

FEDERICO: Perhaps. The poetry of history's Sundays.

DOCTOR: (*Re-reading*)   'Let Socialism be
>   in the teeth of all conflicts
>   for us a monument struck
>   in common bronze.'

There's a certain energy in the words, I'll admit that. Where do they come from?

FEDERICO: From the future. These lines will be written by a man who will end up, at the age of thirty-seven, killing himself with a bullet in his heart.

DOCTOR: A sad prognosis.

FEDERICO: Yet in that idea is everything which makes sense to me. The Adam of a new world.

(*Fireworks brighter than ever.*)

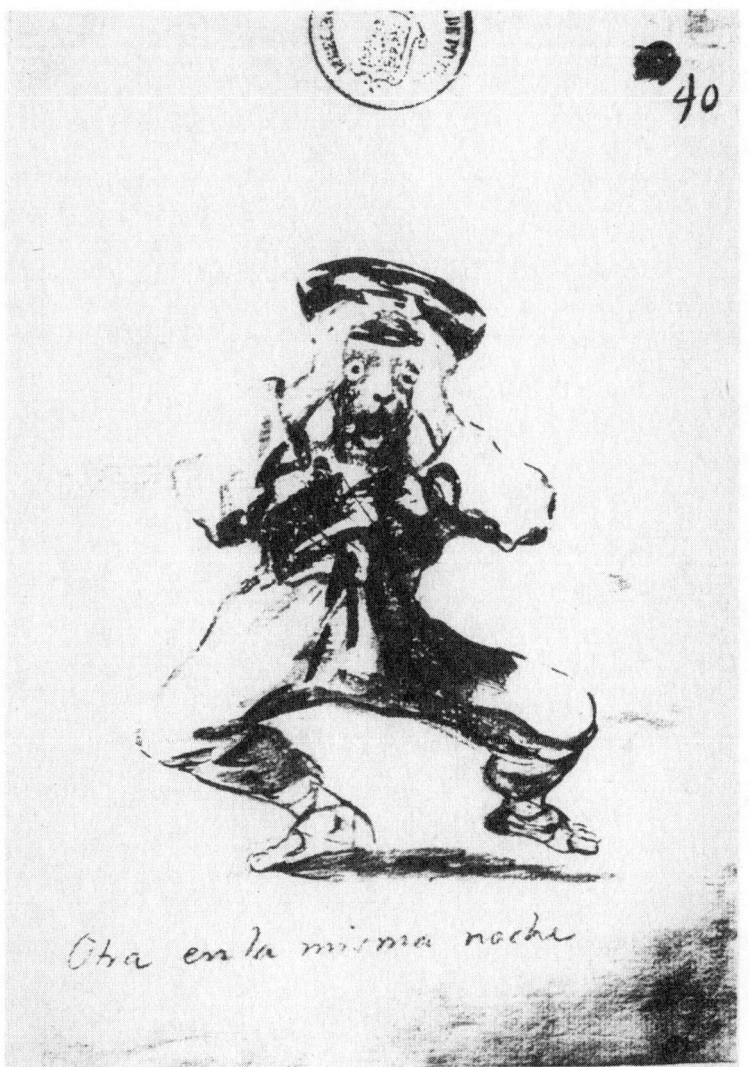

Otra en la misma noche
(drawing for Los Caprichos, The Prado, Madrid)

Night. The cemetery as steppe. GOYA *and* DWARF *are trying to sleep between the rocks.*

DWARF: The Tinker liked his portrait.

GOYA: What did the animals do to deserve being punished by the arrival of man? Did they sleep too much before? Did they repeat the same things too much over and over again? Didn't they make good enough theatre – the animals for the giants?

DWARF: It saved our lives your portrait of the Tinker.

GOYA: The giants got bored and so they had the idea of inventing man for their entertainment.

DWARF: Animals may be dumb but they're not stupid. The only difference is: they don't like stories. And we – we like nothing else but stories. They kill us, they torture us, they drive us mad, our stories, and we live off them. Meanwhile our stories make the giants laugh, they break their ribs. And who makes them laugh the most? I do. Amore, the Dwarf. They started laughing as soon as I dropped out of my mother's belly – they saw the comedy before I'd opened my eyes. You don't make the giants laugh much, Don Francisco, you are too similar. You take after them.

GOYA: I can still hear the dog howling, the same dog.

DWARF: You've got better ears than I have.

GOYA: Can't you hear it?

DWARF: Yes. I can hear your dog.

GOYA: You're lying again, you can hear nothing.

DWARF: I hear, they hear, you don't hear. So what? I want to sleep and you're becoming a pain in the arse with your lies and your exaggerations. And your truth! You are possessed by the truth, Don Francisco. And I'll tell you something else. Truth is dead and buried. No one remembers when or how it happened. But it has happened.

GOYA: What?

DWARF: Buried, yes, like your sardine, covered with muck and stiff and full of worms, your sardine of a truth.

GOYA: Tomorrow we must look for a mule.

DWARF: If we don't wake up with our throats cut.

GOYA: I have told you before not to exaggerate.

DWARF: It happens.

GOYA: I can't hear. If our throats are cut, we don't wake up. If we do wake up, you look for a mule.

ACT TWO

SCENE 7

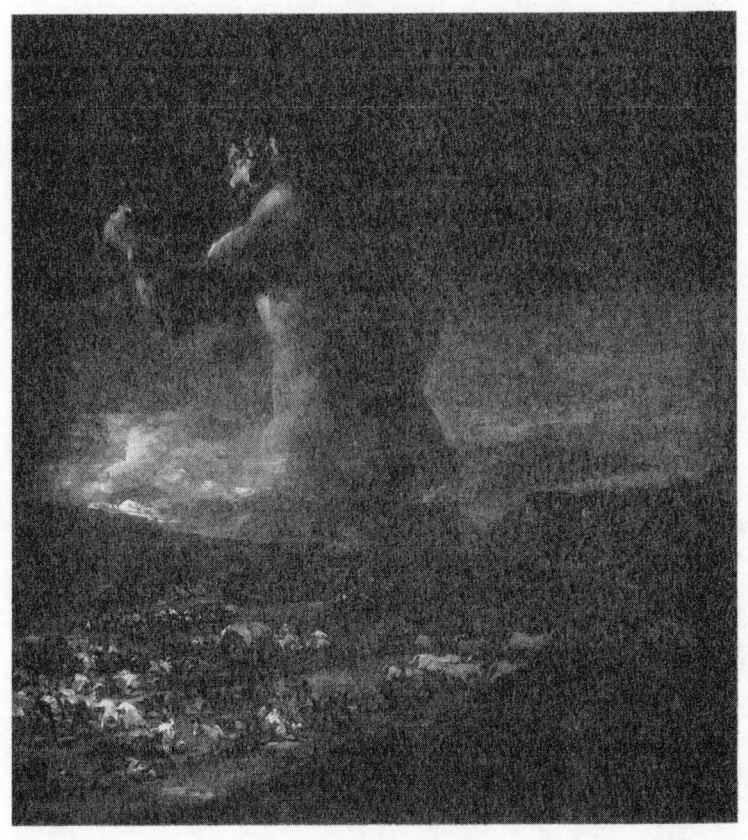

The Collossus
(The Prado, Madrid)

Grey day (1811). The cemetery arranged as a room in Goya's house, Madrid. A large elegant table. Curtains either side of a tall window giving on to the street. A mirror with a gilded frame. A large indoor potted plant. The DOCTOR, *exhausted, sprawls in a chair. Right of stage* GARDENER *is hanging prints to dry on a clothes line. (They look like large white stiff handkerchiefs. The printing is on the other side. We see nothing of the image.)* DWARF *is looking out of the window, as though at a television screen.*

DWARF: It looks to me like the same dog. The one who comes out of his head. The dog who hurts him so much, with orange eyes. Yes, it's the same dog.
   (DOCTOR *comes to end of table, on which lies a sheep's head and two sides of mutton, as in a butcher's shop.*)
DOCTOR: This meat is bad. Indisputably bad and should be thrown away. I thought I could smell it from the chair over there.
GARDENER: He insists. He says he needs it.
DWARF: The dog is following an old woman carrying a bundle.
DOCTOR: Famine in Madrid, the price of bread going up each week – a loaf now costs 30 centimos, that's three times the price of a pass with a tart.
DWARF: Don't exaggerate. I've learnt that. Nothing is to be exaggerated, Doctor. The street smells of sulphur. I can smell it through the window.
GARDENER: (*Hanging another paper*) Twelve copies of 'They don't know what they are doing'. He was never clever – I've told him – at titles.
DOCTOR: Clever enough in other ways though. You have to be clever to let meat rot like this. Enough meat for a dozen people! A baturro never changes. The Duchess was right. They're like mules. Two months ago they were burning their own crops to prevent them falling into the hands of the French. Today they're starving. A visceral irresponsibility.

GARDENER: He won't let anyone remove it.

DWARF: The woman with the bundle and another woman are coming to beg at the door.

GARDENER: He won't be long now. He's putting the finishing touches to a portrait.

DOCTOR: Portrait!

GARDENER: A portrait of General Nicolas Guye.

DOCTOR: The job never stops, does it? (*Knocks on door of Goya's studio.*) Bubonic plague on the outskirts of the city, no road open anywhere, cholera, typhus . . . and you are putting the finishing touches to a portrait! The world is slipping into hell and you are finishing a portrait. On the day before the Last Judgement narcissism reaches its apogee.

DWARF: The two old women have gone away with nothing. One of them is taking off her shawl. She's not old. She's simply not hungry enough yet to prostitute herself. Next week she'll come in mantilla and garters.

(*Enter* GOYA *from studio carrying General's brocaded military tunic which he throws on the table beside the meat.*)

GOYA: Why do you make so much noise?

DOCTOR: (*Shouting*) You should get rid of that meat, it can breed infection in a time of pestilence. Do you understand what I say?

(GOYA *hangs tunic over edge of table, picks up the sheep's head and places it in the collar of the tunic. He steps back to look at the effect.*)

I've come to offer you my congratulations. Congratulations on the honour you've just received from the Court.

GOYA: Pasture is to sheep what air is to birds and water to fish.

GARDENER: He hears what he wants now. Nothing else.

DOCTOR: I want to congratulate you on receiving from the Emperor Joseph Bonaparte the Royal Order of Spain.

GOYA: Sheep believe pasture is not only their sustenance but also their protection. When they flee, they believe the pasture will protect them with its infinite distance. When they charge over a cliff, they do so in trust not fear.

DOCTOR: It's my duty to insist, my friend, that you wash your hands now.

(*Enter* FEDERICO, *wearing the red sash and star of the Royal Order of Spain.*)

FEDERICO: (*To* GOYA) I'm wearing it for you! We're twins.

DWARF: In the street they call it the Order of the Aubergine. They say too that Joseph Bonaparte sits astride a cucumber not a horse.

GOYA: I painted Juan Antonio Llorente wearing his. That's enough for me.

FEDERICO: There are honours we could do without, aren't there, Paco?

DOCTOR: In times like these you have to keep your hands clean.
(FEDERICO *takes off sash and slumps in chair.*)

FEDERICO: The Royal Order!

DWARF: Two French soldiers coming down the street . . .

FEDERICO: (*Pensive in chair*) Who decides who is to survive?

GOYA: I have a favour to ask you.

DOCTOR: Any service I can offer. I have my instruments and phials with me – they're downstairs. Don't hesitate. We've done everything. We've looked up the arses of Bonapartes. We've curetted duchesses –
(GOYA *seizes* DOCTOR's *throat with one hand. His words stop. No one notices except* GARDENER *who passes* GOYA *one of the pegs from the line on which the prints hang.* GOYA *clamps the peg on* DOCTOR's *mouth.*)

DWARF: Two young ladies have approached the French soldiers. With my expert eye I'd give their fathers an income of at least two thousand reales.

GOYA: (*To* DOCTOR) You're going to sign my will. It needs a witness.
(GOYA *unclamps peg.*)

DOCTOR: You are not well, Francisco, you are on the brink of one of your crises. So I will forgive you.

DWARF: One lady is twirling her shoes on her foot. They've settled for a loaf of bread for the two of them.

FEDERICO: (*Looking at etchings*) One, two, three, four, five . . . Each one practically the same. You followed my advice. Remember, Paco? The day they arrested me.

DWARF: An old man has fallen against a wall. He can't get up.

GOYA: (*To* FEDERICO) You look tired. Your forehead looks tired.

FEDERICO: There's no other way, Paco. To pull ourselves out of two centuries of stagnation, to come out of the dungeon, out of the interrogation chamber, the cellar, the graveyard, the secret office – to come out of the blackness into the first light, the very first light; others will come later at noon to follow us. We are right. But we are so alone. We who want to be fathers are like orphans. Can you hear me?

DWARF: The dog is foraging the old man who fell down.

GOYA: The season when they shear the sheep in Aragon and pick the first apricots. The third of May. From that hill, behind the cemetery, you can see at night the lights of the city below. Down there the children are sleeping and my wife is watching the door, biting her fist, waiting for me to return. Up here the French are shooting us one by one. Blindly, deafly. They don't even have to take aim. Their muzzles are so close. Every one of us is waiting to die. Anselmo Ramirez de Arellano, Juan Martinez, Antonio Mazias, Mendez Villamil, Antonio Zambrano . . .

FEDERICO: Stop, Paco! It doesn't suit you. It sounds like a litany.

DWARF: The dead cart's coming with its bell. He can't hear it.

FEDERICO: If our people instead of the French had been in command on your third of May, Francisco, the reprisals would have been even worse. Do you know what Antonio head of our city junta said? I have a terrible memory for words. 'Thank God,' said Antonio when he heard of the executions on the Montana del Principe Pio. 'Thank God there is still at least one army in the world who can hold down a mob!'

GOYA: Out of my sight! Finish! One, two, three. The third man to die is wearing a white shirt and trousers the yellow of lemons. He's falling. Between the order to fire – *Feu!* – and the end of a life, there's time to foresee everything.

(GOYA, *back to the audience, looks towards the window. In it appears a man, face contorted, arms outstretched, wearing a white shirt and lemon trousers.*)

DWARF: Two men have kicked the dog away and are taking off the boots of the old man who is dead.

GOYA: I do not know who chooses what I see. Not me, dear God, not me.

(GOYA *takes his head in his hands and walks like a blind man towards the window. The figure disappears. Only* GOYA *has seen the figure.* GARDENER *takes* GOYA'*s arm and leads him through the door to the studio.*)

(*To* GARDENER *as they leave*) There's a terrible noise in my head. Like water. Like water, unstuck from the earth and drawn by the moon . . . prepare me a canvas for tomorrow. Three hundred and fifty by two hundred and seventy.

DOCTOR: He has these attacks. There's nothing to be done. Just leave him to paint!

(FEDERICO *is seized by a coughing fit.*)

FEDERICO: Can you stop this?

DWARF: The first man has run off with the old man's boots. The second man is chasing after him.

DOCTOR: At night if one can't sleep and one is alone, coughing is almost inevitable. One needs a lady, preferably one with a smooth skin and a good circulation. Caressing is the best cure for nocturnal coughing. The material of the sheets can play a role too.

FEDERICO: (*Between coughs*) It's not night yet and I'm coughing. (*Enter* GOYA *with paper, followed by* GARDENER. *He has recovered his equilibrium.*)

GOYA: Here's the will. Apart from a few bequests to friends, it makes over everything to my wife and my one remaining child, Xavier. I want them to have the wherewithal to be secure. You sign here.

DOCTOR: Your optimism amazes me! In times like ours an inheritance can promise nothing.

GOYA: I can't hear. Please sign.

GARDENER: (*To* FEDERICO) In times like ours, trees, I have noticed, live longer than laws.

FEDERICO: (*Still coughing*) We are planting the Tree of Liberty, mia amigo. One day those who till the land will own it.

GOYA: I like to think of Xavier's children lacking for nothing.

DWARF: It's begun to rain. Everyone's running for shelter. The wind has blown a wet paper, which is sticking on to the face of an old man who is dead. The dog's come back.

ACT TWO

SCENE 8

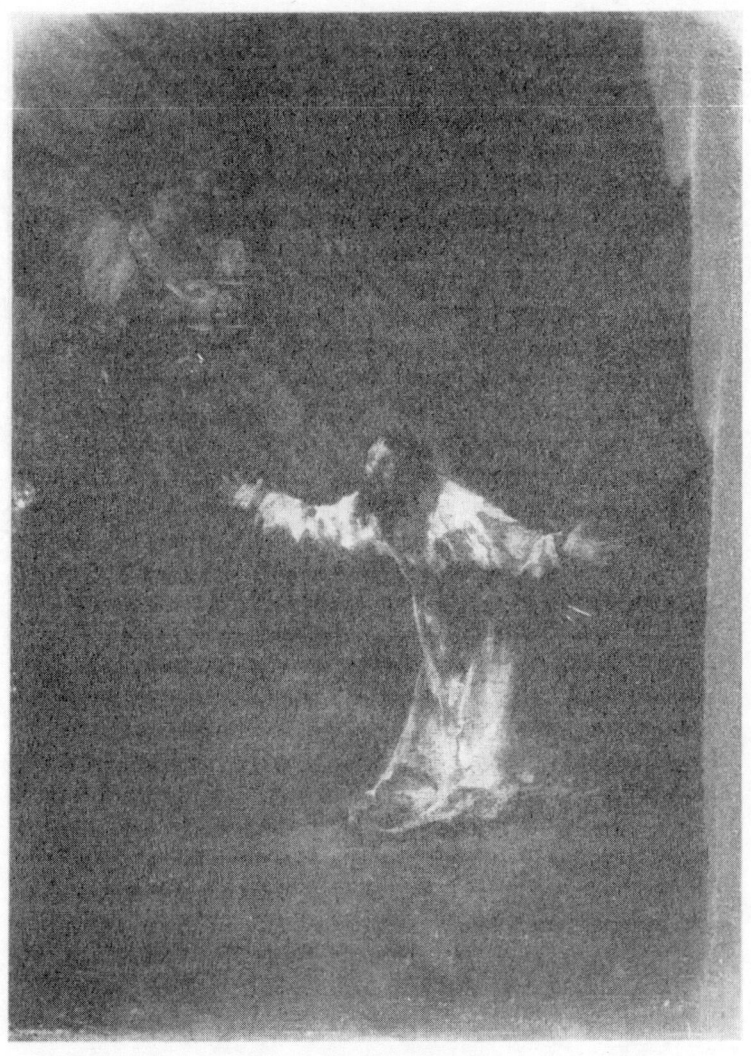

Christ on the Mount of Olives
(Church of San Antonio, Madrid)

Night (1811). The same as previous scene except that the line, on which prints are pegged, now crosses the whole room. GOYA *is fingering the prints on the line.* GARDENER *is splitting wood with an axe for the fire.*

GARDENER: I brought in the barosma plants this morning. I've
    never known such cold so early. I was a bit frightened for
    them.
GOYA: Frightened for what?
GARDENER: The barosma plants.
GOYA: In God's name what are they?
GARDENER: The little bushes in pots with white flowers. The
    ones in the courtyard.
GOYA: White, did you say?
    (GARDENER *nods.*)
    Blind! All of you. You're blind! The flowers you're
    frightened for are pink. Not white. White, if you must, but
    stained with blood. Stop! Don't move your arms. Keep the
    axe there, Juan.
    (GARDENER, *with axe raised above his head, freezes.* GOYA
    continues to examine prints.)
GARDENER: If you need a drawing, Don Francisco, better do it
    quickly.
GOYA: Keep the axe there! Drawing! Drawings come by
    themselves. You just untie the sack, lift it up, tip it, and out
    pours the debris. Drawings are debris. Don't move, Juan.
GARDENER: I have to now.
GOYA: I thought you were strong. I thought you had the
    shoulders of a bull.
GARDENER: There's a louse in my armpit.
GOYA: Don't move. Which one? I'll find it for you.
GARDENER: The left.
    (GOYA *pulls up* GARDENER's *shirt, searches, spectacles on the
    end of nose.*)

GOYA: Can see nothing! Need a candle.

GARDENER: (*Starting to laugh*) It's tickling.

(GOYA *steps back*. GARDENER *lowers axe and splits wood*.)

GOYA: I wanted to give the log at your feet a little more time.

GARDENER: In the circumstances a double cruelty.

(GOYA *doesn't understand*. GARDENER *takes paper from table and writes on it:* DOUBLE CRUELTY.)

GOYA: If logs could see, if they had eyes, if they could count minutes, it would be better for the axe to descend immediately. But logs can't count.

GARDENER: You've never heard what they call men in Malaga?

GOYA: Men?

GARDENER: They call a man a log with nine holes!

(GOYA *counts the holes*.)

GOYA: Did you find any rice today?

GARDENER: No. The French took everything before leaving, and what they didn't take the British have pillaged. Either that or people don't want to sell to us any more. They look dangerous when I ask. In my opinion, Don Francisco, we should prepare to go into hiding. Only the illness of Doña Josefa has prevented me saying this before. I know a place where we can go.

(GOYA *appears not to have heard*. GARDENER *writes on paper:* HIDING?)

GOYA: There's not the slightest cause for alarm. I've already offered my services to the victors. Conquerors need painters and sculptors. Never forget that. Victory is ephemeral – as ephemeral as played music. Victory pictures are like wedding pictures, except there's no bride present. The bride is their own triumph. I don't know why, but it has always been so throughout history. So they want mother-fucking portraits of themselves with their invisible bride. And I can do these portraits like no one else can. I have a weakness for victors – above all for their collars, their boots, their victory robes. I think we were all meant to be triumphant. Before there was any destiny, we were children of a triumph. We were all born of an ejaculation.

(*Enter* DOCTOR.)

DOCTOR: Your wife is asking to see you. I have one thing more to
say to my husband, she says.

(*Exit* DOCTOR *hurriedly*.)

GOYA: Soon I'll do the Duke of Wellington. He insists upon a
horse.

GARDENER: Don Federico has already gone into hiding.

GOYA: When the Whore's Desired One returns to sit on our
throne, I shall paint him with a sword under his hand and a
cocked hat under his arm. And if he won't sit for me, I'll
paint him from memory. (*Looks in mirror*.) Everyone will
forgive me.

GARDENER: The washerwomen say you're not so deaf you don't
hear the clink of reales in the money bags. That's how you
know when to change sides, they say.

GOYA: Everyone will forgive me.

(*Enter* DOCTOR.)

DOCTOR: I regret to have to tell you, Don Francisco, it's too late.
Your wife is dead.

(GOYA *falls to his knees*.)

GOYA: Even my wife will forgive me.

(GOYA *remains kneeling with bowed head. Imperceptible sound
of the sea. Abruptly he scrambles to his feet*.)

If only men didn't forgive!

(GOYA *grasps the clothes line with both hands and walks beside
it, holding it like a man in a gale*.)

Do you know how much is unforgivable? Do you know there
are acts which can never be forgiven? Nobody sees them.
Not even God.

(*Sea becomes louder*.)

The perpetrators bury what they do from themselves and
others with words. They call their victims names, they fasten
labels to them, they repeat stories. Everything is prepared by
curses and insults and whispering and speeches and chatter.
The Devil works with words. He has no need of anything
else. He distributes words and with the innocent working of
the tongue and the roof of the mouth and the vocal cords,
people talk themselves into evil, and afterwards with the
same words and the same wicked numbers they hide what

they've done, so it's forgotten, and what is forgotten is forgiven.

(GOYA *comes to a print.*)

What is engraved doesn't forgive.

(GOYA *falls to his knees.*)

Do not forgive us, O Lord. Let us see the unforgivable so we may never forget it.

(GOYA *somehow gets to his feet, walks to exit where* DOCTOR *entered.*)

Forgive me, Josefa, forgive me . . .

ACT THREE

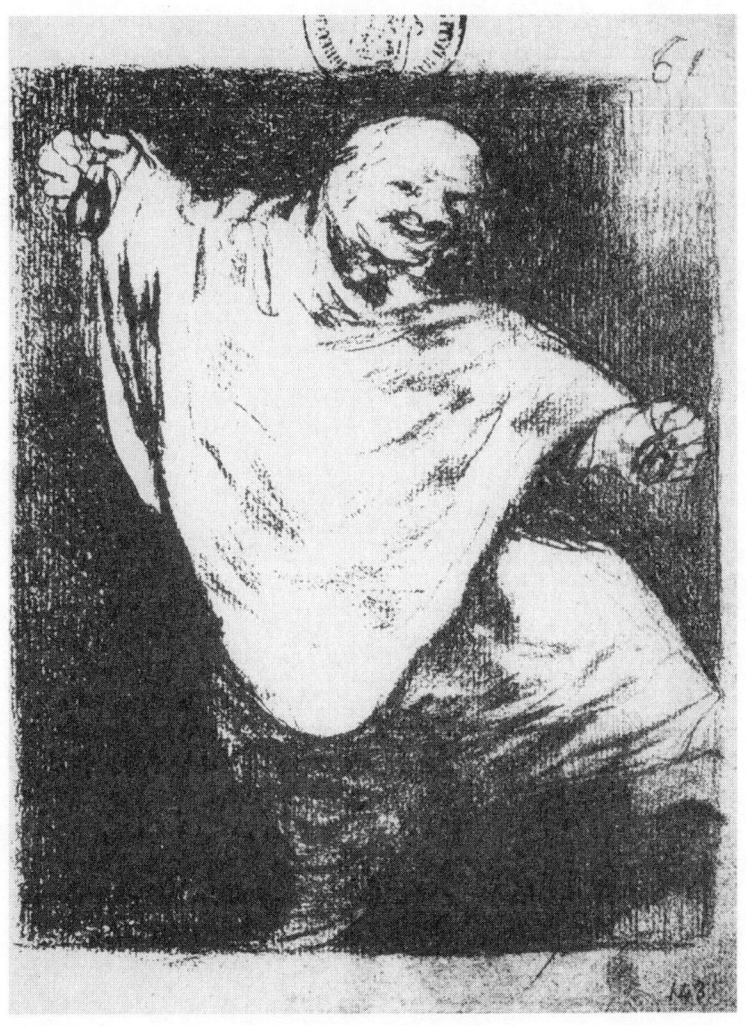

Fantasma con castanuelas
(The Prado, Madrid)

Early spring morning (1827/8). Sunshine. The garden of Goya's house in Bordeaux. (The scene is almost identical with that of the cemetery.) GARDENER *on ladder is pruning a vine against a wall. Enter* GOYA *with stick (now over eighty), accompanied by* FEDERICO *(same age).*

GOYA: (*Pointing*) There's a Goldfinch, there in the almond tree – do you see him?

FEDERICO: I tell you every morning, Francisco, my eyes are failing.

(*The two old men stand still.* GOYA *imitates song of Goldfinch.*)

GOYA: That's how he sings, Goldfinch.

FEDERICO: How do you know?

GOYA: (*Not hearing*) Would you like to hear Nut Hatch? Pepa teaches me. Bird by bird she teaches me their songs.

FEDERICO: Your new painting?

GOYA: Two centuries ago in Amsterdam a Dutchman painted Goldfinch.

FEDERICO: (*Shouting*) How's the new painting?

GOYA: Sky's wrong behind the head. Never had trouble with a sky before.

FEDERICO: French skies are not the same. Look at it. Milky. French bakeries are different too. With age, I regret to say, I find myself from time to time becoming greedy.

(FEDERICO *takes a brioche out of his pocket, offers half to* GOYA. *They sit.*)

GOYA: Have you said yet: 'With age, I regret to say, I find myself from time to time becoming greedy'?

(FEDERICO *throws crumbs to the birds.*)

I slept better this night. No dreams. That's why you arrived before I was up.

FEDERICO: Didn't matter. I had plenty to think about . . . there are spies from the Holy Office sent here to Bordeaux. I'm sure of it. Don Tiburcio has refused to give us any more money for the paper.

GOYA: Which one?

FEDERICO: Our paper in Spanish – the one I edit.

GOYA: I'll do a lithograph for you.

FEDERICO: The only explanation is that they threatened to maltreat Don Tiburcio's family in Valencia. Meanwhile we owe three hundred to the printer.

GOYA: Soon there'll be more exile papers in the world than stars in the sky.

FEDERICO: Just three hundred to pay the printer.

GOYA: My lithographs aren't selling. People don't want to know. They want everything in colour and stereo . . . What's the latest news from our country?

FEDERICO: The latest! The dark ages. The Constitution annulled and void. Thought manacled. People disappearing in the streets. Torture. Electric shocks. Underground garages. The gluttony of terror. The same as I tell you every morning, my friend. Will anybody ever bring news of a different sort? The latest, Paco, is that we're already living in the future. Not the one we fought and died for. The one the giants substituted for ours . . . That's the latest. Will it ever be different?

GOYA: If you're quiet for a moment, I'll do Nightingale.

FEDERICO: If I didn't know better, Frogman, I'd say you'd gone simple.

GOYA: Then don't ask simple questions like: 'Will anybody ever bring news of a different sort?'

FEDERICO: So you heard me?

GOYA: Of course not.

FEDERICO: Everywhere the restoration of the past. Everywhere boasts about what was once thought shameful. (*Shouting*) Tell me what's left of our hopes.

GOYA: This! (*Imitates Goldfinch.*) What's left of our hopes is a long despair which will engender new hopes. Many, many hopes . . . I'm going to live to be as old as Titian.
(*Enter* PEPA.)

PEPA: Your hot chocolate is waiting in the house.

FEDERICO: Everything should be clear, except hot chocolate which should be thick.

GOYA: Has he said it again?

102

(PEPA *nods and takes* GOYA's *arm. Exit* FEDERICO *and*
GARDENER, *carrying ladder, towards house.* PEPA *and* GOYA
*walk slowly towards swing. They speak softly, almost
whispering.* GOYA *has no difficulty in hearing.*)
Have you read the pages I marked of Francisco de Quevedo y
Villegas?

PEPA: All of them.

GOYA: And?

PEPA: They were about the Last Judgement.

GOYA: And the story about me?

PEPA: The painter Hieronymus Bosch finds himself in hell and
there he's cross-questioned. When you were a painter on the
earth, they ask him, why did you paint so many deformed
men? And Hieronymus replies to them: Because I don't
believe in Devils.

GOYA: Correct.

(PEPA *sits on the swing.* GOYA *stands before her.*)
Do you know who is the favourite in the asylum down by the
river? Napoleon! I counted fifteen men wearing hats, and on
the hats scraps of paper with the words 'I am Napoleon'
written on them. Do you know why Napoleon appeals to the
mad?

PEPA: No.

GOYA: Because Napoleon was mad enough to boast, 'I have an
annual income of three hundred thousand men!'

(PEPA *picks some flowers, offers them to* GOYA.)

PEPA: On Friday at 2 p.m. in the Place d'Aquitaine, there will be
a public execution, with the guillotine, French style.

GOYA: I shall be there.

PEPA: A poor wretch called Jean Bertain who murdered his
brother-in-law.

GOYA: Perhaps the brother-in-law was raping his niece. Amongst
men pity is rare.

PEPA: When you feel pity, you close your eyes.

GOYA: I have eyes in the back of my head. They never close. Do
you love me a little?

PEPA: A little, a lot, passionately?

GOYA: If I painted a miniature on ivory it could hang between your breasts. Am I mad, Pepa?

PEPA: You don't imagine you're a Napoleon.

(GOYA *sits on a stool, takes his head in his hands.*)

GOYA: A man bends double between a pair of lips. He tries to get into the mouth. When he is in, it's very difficult for him to get out. One must name everything one sees for what it is. Never stop looking at consequences. The only chance against barbarism. To see consequences.

PEPA: Don't torture yourself, Francisco. It happens at the end of the morning – and it passes, it goes away. Let's play together. In our family album (*Opens a book on her knees*) I put a picture of a young man. He's wearing a large black hat and he has dark piercing eyes.

GOYA: Doubtless he was very ambitious.

PEPA: Large, sensuous mouth. Strong appetites.

GOYA: In our family album I put a picture of a man standing before an easel.

PEPA: Around the brim of his hat there are candles.

GOYA: He worked all night.

PEPA: Quel panache! He has very smart, tight trousers. And now the same man, older. He's wearing glasses.

GOYA: He'd seen too much.

PEPA: He has a good complexion and he has a white silk scarf round his neck.

GOYA: It was already the year of the French Revolution.

PEPA: In our family album I put a picture of a man standing against a blackness. He looks stunned – stunned by the fact he's still alive.

GOYA: He's simply old – almost seventy. Madrid is infected by the plague and it has killed Amore.

PEPA: The expression changes but it's always the same man.

GOYA: It's perhaps the same man. But it's not me.

PEPA: Yes, it's you and it's your art, you painted the pictures.

(*Suddenly* GOYA *loses interest. He is staring hard at the Duchess of Alba's grave beyond the swing. The* DUCHESS *appears.* PEPA *cannot see her.*)

GOYA: Leave me now, Pepa.

PEPA: Your art, Don Francisco.

GOYA: To hell with my art!

PEPA: You were a prophet. In your art you foresaw the future.

> (DUCHESS *advances towards* GOYA.)

GOYA: Come, come.

PEPA: With such compassion . . .

GOYA: Get out, I tell you, fuck off.

> (GOYA *chases* PEPA *out of the garden with his stick. He turns to the audience.*)

Voyeurs! Fuck off!

> (*His back to audience, he watches* DUCHESS *undress for him, as in a striptease.*)

My darling life.

> (DUCHESS *opens her arms to him.*)

DUCHESS: Everything is for you, every feather. Come, my love, come, come, my frogman.

> (DUCHESS *disappears.* GOYA *falls in a heap on to the ground. The stage is silent. As if the curtain should now come down but the mechanism doesn't work.* PEPA *enters, sits on the ground, places* GOYA*'s head on her lap.*)

PEPA: Every time you do the same thing. She always escapes from you. You're never quick enough.

GOYA: I walk on sticks . . .

> (*Enter from different directions all other actors, dressed as they were in the Prologue.* GARDENER, *masked, goes over to beehive.* PEPA *gently disengages herself from* GOYA, *gets to her feet and rings the bell. The actors begin to leave the cemetery exactly as in the Prologue.* PEPA *rejoins* GOYA.)

WIDOW: (*To herself*) Let a little justice come to this earth, dear Lord.

DOCTOR: (*To* ACTRESS) You wanted to seduce your father so you became an actress.

GOYA: (*To* PEPA) Have they finished? Is my portrait done?

PEPA: Yes, it's done.

GOYA: They must sign it.

PEPA: It's done.

GOYA: Am I dead, Pepa?

PEPA: Don't worry. For tonight you're well and truly dead.

> (LEANDRO *is the last to leave.*)

LEANDRO: (*Shouting to* PEPA) Wear your new white dress!
GOYA: That's good . . .
    (GOYA *closes his eyes and sleeps.* GARDENER *blows smoke into hive. White curtain, without image or signature, descends.*)

A Question of Geography

To the memory of
Yevgeniya Semyonouna Ginzburg

June–August, 1952

We chose this moment because it was one of relative quiet, of routine; ten months before Stalin's death. The last massive wave of arrests had been in 1949. Things were returning to 'normal'. The trauma of the war was a few years away. The economic situation was improving.

Kolyma

Region of the labour camps in the north-east of eastern Siberia, about 250 miles east of Oimiakon, where the coldest winters are regularly recorded. The river Kolyma crosses this mountainous landscape which is rich in seams of gold ore, and flows into the frozen Arctic ocean. The whole region is cut off from the rest of the country by mountains and the vast *taïga*. The only way in or out is by plane or boat. That is why the inhabitants call the rest of Russia 'the mainland' or 'the continent'. Kolyma is not, geographically speaking, an island; but to live there is to be exiled off-shore.

The one large town of the region is Magadan: the capital of the Gulag. (The word *Gulag* is an abbreviation in Russian for State Authority for Camps.) The area, with its capital city, was at that time a state within a state, with its own administration and population, the latter consisting mostly of Zeks, ex-Zeks and their guards, named collectively 'the Bruise'.

Thus Magadan and Kolyma exist in a very real physical sense; but their names also exist in the dreams and the unconscious of the Soviet people. For example, when Vissoski sings in one of his songs: 'I'm through – through with everything and I'm going to catch a plane to Magadan,' the words ignite memories and experiences which are beyond a given place and are larger than any individual. Such words are more than symbols: they form part of a history that has entered a people's soul.

111

Convit
(Combined vitamin.) A concoction made from pine needles, which contain vitamin C, thought to be an antidote against scurvy.

Sudar Lumbercamp
An area in Kolyma where prisoners were sent to fell trees. Given the cold, the lack of food and warm clothing, a stint of work there often proved fatal. Being sent to Sudar was a disciplinary measure, a punishment, meted out particularly to '58s'.

'A 58'
A term used to describe any prisoner, man or woman, condemned under Article 58 of the penal code. This article was interpreted so loosely that it finally covered all prisoners who were not criminals by common law.

Article 58
The 14th paragraph of this article enumerated all activities subject to being considered prejudicial to the interests and security of the state. They ranged from 'spying' to 'terrorism', from 'sabotage' at work to a refusal to denounce other 'traitors'. Under this article anybody could be condemned if picked upon. A '58' was spoken of as 'an enemy of the people'. In the camps they were treated worse than ordinary criminals.

Zek
A popular abbreviation of *zaklioutchonny*, meaning prisoner.

The Bruise
A name invented for the military personnel in charge of the camps. In fact they were known as 'Vokhra' which is an abbreviation from *Voorujonnaïa Okhrana*, meaning armed guards. For us *the Bruise* also includes those who worked for the KGB (Committee of State Security). The latter wore blue insignia on their uniforms. From this blue came the colour of the bruise.

A Decembrist
After the mutiny of officers against the Czar on 25 December

1825, in St Petersburg, the term *Decembrist* came to mean a revolutionary or idealist. Pushkin celebrated them in his poetry.

The Taïga

This is very different from the steppe. It refers to the enormous Siberian forest area which supplied wood for the whole of the Soviet Union. In Stalin's time nearly all this wood was felled by prisoners. Nothing romantic resided in the word *taïga*.

NELLA BIELSKI

ERNST MOISSEEVITCH OIZERMANN
Nicknamed 'Eric' by Daria. Forty-six years old, thin, with curly white hair. Limps slightly. He wears a worn, shiny suit. Metal spectacles. He carries everywhere a battered, leather medical bag. His situation in Magadan is unlike that of any of the other characters. He is still a prisoner in the Zone, but, because he is a doctor who treats the guard officers, he has a right to come into the town during the afternoons.

DARIA PETROVNA PETROVA
Abbreviation: 'Dacha'. Thirty-eight years old. She is not particularly beautiful, but she has a strong, reassuring presence. The reassurance she gives has a lot to do with her gestures. She was arrested in 1937 and served ten years in the Zone. Now she is in permanent forced residence in the town of Magadan. She works in one of the town's infant schools. Dacha and Ernst met in the Zone. They live, as best they can, as a couple.

SACHA
Sixteen years old. The son of Dacha. He was one and a half when his mother was arrested. He has been brought up in Leningrad by Dacha's sister, Katya. Like all boys of his age – and despite his size and adult appearance – he reveals a mixture of maturity and childishness.

GRICHA
Sixty years old, bald, agile – with something of the conjurer about him, something of the fox. He has seen more of the Zone than anyone else. Now in Forced Residence. He works as a porter in the special stores for the Bruise. (The Bruise is the term used to designate guards, officers and all Zone administrators.)

IGOR ISSAIEVITCH GERTZMANN
Fifty-five years old. Once a violinist of great talent. His body,

although aged and worn, still suggests this. He wears a quilted coat and canvas trousers – almost the same as he wore as a Zek in the Zone. In Forced Residence.

LYDIA IVANOVNA
Forty-three years old. Slightly over-dressed – in hand-me-down clothes. An economist by training. Worked, before being arrested, in the planning section of a textile factory. An amateur 'expert' of literature and poetry.

MICHA
Thirty years old. He was in the Zone as a criminal, not as a political prisoner. Now works as a lorry driver. Is free to leave and return to the Continent.

UNKNOWN YOUNG WOMAN
Between twenty-two and twenty-five years old.

BRUISE 1
Forty years old. A little tired and slack in his duties.

BRUISE 2
Younger than Bruise 1. Handsome, tall, zealous.

A Question of Geography is set in Dacha's room, in Magadan, the principal town of Kolyma. It covers the period June–August 1952.

A Question of Geography was first performed in French by The
National Theatre of Marseille in 1985 at the Theatre of the Criée,
and, later, at the Odéon in Paris. It was first performed in English
by the Royal Shakespeare Company at The Other Place,
Stratford-upon-Avon, in 1987. The cast included:

ERNST MOISSEEVITCH OIZERMANN	Clive Russell
DARIA PETROVNA PETROVA (DACHA)	Harriet Walter
SACHA	Linus Roache
GRICHA	Jimmy Gardner
IGOR ISSAIEVITCH GERTZMANN	John Carlisle
LYDIA IVANOVNA	Susan Colverd
MICHA	Peter Polycarpou
UNKNOWN YOUNG WOMAN	Sonia Ritter
Director	John Caird
Designer	Sue Blane

117

ACT ONE

SCENE ONE

June 1952. Evening. It is still light. (Outside, the white night of the Arctic.) A room in an apartment house in the port of Magadan, principal town of Kolyma. The room, on the ground floor, is large and very simply furnished, but one senses in it the presence of a woman. On the left a window, on the right the door on to the street, two beds, a table, a sink. DACHA – apron, chignon, wearing glasses – is reading a book at the table. There is food ready on the table: potatoes, herring, black bread. A lamp, shaded with an orange scarf. DACHA is waiting. On a massive primus stove a 50-litre saucepan of water is simmering. On the floor is a zinc bath. DACHA looks up towards the door, then at a large alarm clock. We hear the tick-tick loudly. ERNST opens the door with his own key and enters. DACHA takes off her glasses and watches him come towards her. He limps slightly. He places on the table a string bag with two newspaper packages inside it. Then he opens his case and takes out a stethoscope, and an old instrument for taking blood pressure. DACHA rolls up her sleeve. No word has yet been spoken. He takes her blood pressure. Meticulously.

ERNST: Sixteen. It was seventeen yesterday, no?
DACHA: On Monday I had nineteen.
ERNST: I want to keep it at sixteen. For a 58/11, aged 38, that's not bad. (*Puts away his instruments, goes to wash his hands.*) Six terminal cases today. Three scurvys, sent to the hospital, and two TBs. It's a good omen. The Bruise may be getting more human.
DACHA: Perhaps good omens are still possible. Who knows?
ERNST: A 58/10 will probably die during the night. If I can manage some sleep . . .
DACHA: You have to sleep. Who is he?
ERNST: A poet.
DACHA: You saw his file?
ERNST: Yes, I remember his name – Serebriakov.
DACHA: (*Nodding*) Pavel Serebriakov.

ERNST: (*Unwrapping the newspaper packages in the string bag*)
Look, some greengroceries.

DACHA: Not a present from the poet!

ERNST: (*A little grimace*) They're straight from the Agrobase.
The Colonel called me out again this afternoon. His daughter
has measles. Mother and Father were beside themselves;
they thought their little daughter had scarlet fever. I
reassured them. So they gave me a lettuce.

(ERNST *eats the bread for a moment without speaking.* DACHA
*watches him, as she does every evening, listening to the recital of
his day.*)

As for the Colonel, since his arrival, there are two conflicting
points of view about him. Some say he is scrupulous but
sadistic; others say he is sadistic but scrupulous! I don't take
sides. By his little daughter's bedside he fusses like a hen.
My diagnosis of measles earned me the lettuce and radishes.

DACHA: The Colonel is generous!

(ERNST *finishes eating and is more relaxed. He comes behind*
DACHA *and puts his hands on her shoulders. She leans her head
back against his chest.*)

ERNST: Twelve visits in the town this evening. Eleven of them for
nothing. The twelfth had cirrhosis of the liver. A sergeant
of twenty-five, drinking himself to death. I warned the Colonel
that in the Zone Operating Theatre we have no gauze left. We
have to sterilize rags. I told him even twenty kilograms of gauze
would be something to go on with. It'll make no difference.

DACHA: (*Smiling*) And do you know what I want to go on with?

ERNST: What?

DACHA: Twelve square metres of hardboard.

ERNST: What?

DACHA: And if that's not possible, twelve square metres of thick
cardboard.

ERNST: Nobody could say you lack imagination, my love.
(ERNST *starts to undress. His white body is badly scarred.*
DACHA *pours water into the bath.*)

DACHA: You have teeth like Gary Cooper.

ERNST: Thanks to the pine needles! By the way, *convit* is no
longer obligatory, a new order from Moscow.

DACHA: You'll always be the most beautiful man in my life, and the pines have nothing to do with it.
(ERNST, *naked, walks over towards the window.*)
ERNST: What's the hardboard for?
DACHA: Patience, doctor, patience. Everything in good time. Come.
(ERNST *sits in the bath.* DACHA *soaps and washes him.*)
The last time I saw Sacha I was bathing him. There was a knock at the door. I wiped my hands on the apron. (*Imitates the gestures.*) There were four of them. What's it for, I asked. I knew what it was for. My own worry was who was going to finish giving Sacha his bath. They're thoughtful, the Bruise; they had already warned the neighbour's wife.
ERNST: And now your Sacha knows *how* to bath himself and doesn't need you for that.
(*She is soaping his hair.*) But me (*laughs*) I do!
(DACHA *pours water over his head. Both are laughing. There is a knock on the door.* DACHA *makes the same gesture with her soapy hands on her apron and goes to half-open the door. A* BRUISE *pushes it wide open.*)
BRUISE I: Citizen Oizermann.
ERNST: (*Sitting in bath, still naked, calm*) Citizen Oizermann present! (*To* DACHA) Give me my glasses. (*Puts them on. To* BRUISE I) What can I do for you?
BRUISE I: You are required to report immediately to the Commandant.
(*He approaches the bath, stiffly.* DACHA *seizes a towel and holds it up like a curtain, so as to hide* ERNST. *The* BRUISE – *ill at ease – ignores the towel.*)
ERNST: You want me to come like this?
(*He stands up, dripping naked.* DACHA *tries to raise the towel higher.*)
BRUISE I: You have five minutes. (*Turns abruptly and strides back to the door.*) The Colonel's daughter has vomited up her supper.
(*The* BRUISE *leaves.* ERNST *steps out of the bath and starts dressing.*)
DACHA: Too much to eat!

ERNST: (*Dressing quickly*) Calm, Dachenka. Don't fret. Why do you want the hardboard?

DACHA: A telegram came today.

ERNST: From whom?

DACHA: Leningrad.

ERNST: Bad news?

DACHA: From Sacha.

ERNST: Sacha!

DACHA: That's why I want the hardboard.

ERNST: Dacha, I have to go, don't talk in riddles.

DACHA: Sacha has taken the decision to come to Magadan.

ERNST: Taken the decision!

DACHA: When the school year is over.

ERNST: This year?

DACHA: In about a week.

ERNST: What time?

DACHA: Eric, he's coming, he's coming here!

ERNST: And the hardboard?

DACHA: To make a room for him in the corner there.

ERNST: It won't happen.

DACHA: (*Still holding the towel in her hands*) I believe he will come.

ERNST: May God protect him and may he never come here!

(ERNST *goes towards the door. Pauses. Takes a wrapped sweet out of his pocket.*)

The Colonel's other child gave me a sweet. (*Pause.*) Keep it for Sacha.

DACHA: It'll be a good summer, Eric, you'll see.

(*Exit* ERNST. DACHA *starts to empty the bath. Stops in mid-action and takes the telegram out of her pocket. Reads it out loud.*)

'Decision taken by Sacha to spend vacation in Magadan. Stop. Letter follows. Stop. Katya.' You were bigger than me, Katya, and more serious and more beautiful, yet you were jealous. You couldn't be jealous of me now, Katinka, could you? It wouldn't be reasonable.

(*She picks up the zinc bath to hang it on the wall. The light from the window is fading.*)

Every time Maman said it was bath time you howled so loud,

Katinka. Papa would come out of his study and say: Be quiet, Miss. The Great Blanqui, Miss, is just about to make his speech to the massed crowd at Bourges on the 15th May 1848, how can I follow such an historical moment with you making this din? How could we know then, Katya, that following historical moments would earn him a bullet in the neck?

(*Through the window a patriotic song sung by passers-by who are drunk. And the voices of a man and woman quarrelling.* DACHA *shuts the window angrily. She picks up the sweet from the table and turns it in her fingers.*)

'Decision taken by Sacha.' So you take decisions, you are almost a man.

(*She sits down on the bed by the door. The light from the window continues to grow fainter. Pause. Ticking of clock.*)

Your father used to come, Sacha, and fetch me after my lectures. He would wait by the bridge and we'd cross it together. He always carried my books. He had very blue eyes, like yours, full of light. He had tiny feet and wore pointed shoes – as if he wanted to have the least contact possible with the ground.

(*Pause. Ticking.*)

He somehow saw us all and the whole history of our planet from way, way above, from where everything fitted together perfectly into circles and the circles into spirals going higher and higher. The great hymn of history!

(*Clock.*)

When I told Papa I was going to marry Serioja, Papa made a joke: So your children will be young Hegelians! How could we know that studying Hegel with passion would lead to six millimetres of pointed steel in the back of the neck.

(*Pause. Ticking.*)

Before we knew that, before they arrested your father, he never liked it when I wore black. When you're very young, wearing black gives you the idea of being a *femme fatale.*

(*Knock on the door. Enter* GRICHA. *He enters the room like a conjuror beginning his act.* DACHA *switches on the lights. He holds a herring wrapped up in paper, as if it were a bouquet of flowers. He embraces* DACHA.)

GRICHA: Hedgehogs are the only animals who make love looking at each other face to face. Don't argue. I've just seen them doing it. My compliments! The only woman of Magadan who stays the same. (*Unwraps the paper to display the herring.*) Fished off Vladivostock! It's not Swedish, it's not Norwegian, it's not Icelandic – this fish was caught in the waters of Holy Russia! Fat, juicy, and the spices, oh, the spices that go with it – cinnamon, bay leaves, cloves, nutmeg, peppercorns – all, like perfumes on the breath of our motherland! Ten barrels full. Do you have a cigarette? I unloaded a ton of tomatoes today. Don't look surprised. If the cases drip, we say they're loaded with tomatoes. (*Still holding the herring*) Take it, sweetheart, it's not a stinging nettle. Grasp it firmly from underneath, move the hand up – never down – and it won't sting.

DACHA: Gricha, haven't you been drinking?

GRICHA: We'll never know when the ball is over.

(*He begins to dance with the herring clutched to his chest.
DACHA intervenes, takes it from him and puts it on the table.*)

DACHA: Better dance with me!

(*They waltz a few steps. Abruptly* GRICHA *steps back.*)

GRICHA: Fuck it! I've never seen you dance before, not even when you got your White Pass.

DACHA: My son's coming.

GRICHA: Children are the flowers of life! And who is the Best Friend of All Children, everywhere?

DACHA: Be quiet!

GRICHA: There! You've given yourself away. No wonder they picked you up and did you with Article 58. You are incorrigible, you refuse his edification – he who is the Best Friend of All Children, the Best Trainer of All Athletes, the Great Linguist.

DACHA: Anyway he's coming.

(GRICHA *takes out of his pocket a small bunch of daisies and places them beside the fish on the table.* DACHA *watches, a little indulgent.* GRICHA *sits on the bed by the door. Suddenly he looks tired. Silence. We hear the clock.*)

GRICHA: You haven't got a cigarette to give me?

(DACHA *finds him one on the shelf with the books*.)

DACHA: Gricha, dear, can you lay your hands on some hardboard and a little door?

GRICHA: You should catch the rabbit before you build the hutch!

DACHA: This rabbit is now sixteen.

GRICHA: And what the fuck is he coming to do here?

DACHA: Everyone tells me the same thing. What's the matter with you all? Even Ernst.

GRICHA: I'm sorry. It was a hard day.

(DACHA *clears the table. A calm.*)

DACHA: How's the pain in your chest, Gricha?

GRICHA: (*Ignoring the question*) You must be wondering how your son will feel about Ernst.

DACHA: I suppose so.

GRICHA: Forget it. More to the point to ask how he will feel about all of us here in the white frozen fog. One should never underestimate the importance of geography.

DACHA: (*Quietly and almost to herself*) If he took the decision – that's what it said – read it!

(*She takes the telegram from her apron pocket and hands it to him. He holds it far away for he is far-sighted.*)

GRICHA: 'Imprudent decision taken by Citizen Dacha, to ignore geography. Stop.'

DACHA: He never knew his father.

GRICHA: Let us consider Ernst as Father Elect. Ernst was born to be a father.

DACHA: Perhaps yes . . .

GRICHA: If you want to have a large family you must know how to count. Counting comes naturally to our Ernst Moisseevitch.

DACHA: (*Very quietly*) I saw him, one spring morning in the Zone, counting the number of leaves on the one and only tree.

GRICHA: It must have been a snowball tree.

DACHA: Why?

GRICHA: 'Where there's a snowball tree, there's always an uncle' as the proverb says. A variety of viburnum . . . And your Sacha, he lives with his uncle?

127

DACHA: Yes, the husband of my sister, Katya. He's an architect who has built two universities.

(*Silence. Clock.* DACHA *goes to the bed behind the curtain and sits down on it to sew. We can see both* DACHA *and* GRICHA *but to each other they are invisible. They speak across the curtain. For a little while they let the silence continue:* DACHA *sewing,* GRICHA *sinking into fatigue.*)

Gricha, why did the Bruise let me go that night at Agrobase number 5?

GRICHA: I told him you had syphillis. And I ought to know! I told him. I made out I was one of your victims.

DACHA: (*Murmuring*) You were my guardian angel.

GRICHA: He didn't want to believe me. He said that on the list of Zeks there was nothing about the clap against your name. It's just happened I told him, since the last examination. And cunt that he was, he believed me.

DACHA: You should have been a diplomat, Gricha, not a porter at the Special Provisions Depot.

GRICHA: You're right and what's more I speak French like a Frenchman. 'Dans l'orient désert quel devint mon ennui!' Racine!

DACHA: They suffered in Racine too . . . At Agrobase 5 I never thought I'd live to see Sacha.

GRICHA: Miracles only happen in this world, Dachinka, not in the next . . . (*Slumps into fatigue and then comes to life again.*) Take the miracle of the Holy Trinity. For two millennia it had them worried, and it is only now at the beginning of the fifties of this century, so full of promise, that your Gricha has discovered the secret. I am my own Father, my own Son and my own Holy Ghost.

DACHA: (*Leaving the bed and approaching him*) I think the Holy Ghost has had enough. Supposing he sleeps here tonight?

GRICHA: Do you know I saw – with my own eyes – two cases of oranges today.

DACHA: Can you get some for Sacha?

GRICHA: There's always a grass about.

DACHA: Don't run the risk, then.

GRICHA: I never run risks. I'm untouchable.

(DACHA *leaves* GRICHA *sitting on the bed. She goes to the mirror and undoes her hair, which falls over her shoulders. She goes to the bed behind the curtain.*)

DACHA: Goodnight, Gricha. Sleep well.

GRICHA: (*Sitting on the bed, his head between his hands*) Goodnight ... Goodnight ... those must be the words they still repeat on the Continent before they are arrested. Goodnight, sweet dreams, the shits of this motherfucking motherland ... sssshhh, Gricha, ssshhh, my little boy, sshh, papa, goodnight, my boy, goodnight, papa, goodnight motherfuckers. (*Takes off his socks and shoes and brings one of his maimed feet to his mouth, kisses it.*) There's the cleverest ... ah! ... the brains of the foot. (*Strokes and cradles one of his feet. Then lies down, murmuring*) Shh! Sshh! Goodnight ... sshh.

(*The lights go down. We hear breathing in the dark.*)

A week later. Evening. The scene unchanged except that in the far left corner a partition with a door has been put up to make a room for Sacha.

MICHA: (*In the doorway, reluctant to enter*) I'll be leaving you here. This is where she lives.

SACHA: (*Entering*) Come in, there's no one here, come in.
(*He looks round the room, surprised and curious.*)

MICHA: You feeling a bit lost, little brother?

SACHA: A bit.

MICHA: Take it easy, they've seen everything here. You'll find a place for yourself.

SACHA: I was meant to arrive tomorrow, you see, that's why there's no one. I came today because tomorrow's flight was cancelled. (*Pause.*) So she lives here. I've seen a photo of her, a marriage photo, but nothing since.

MICHA: In the Zone, kid, there aren't any picture-framers.

SACHA: She has dark eyes and she's not very tall. She'd come up to my chest, I'd say.

MICHA: I've never seen your mother. I've just heard about her. She works at the Infant School.

SACHA: What have you heard?
(*He walks round the room examining the few objects.*)

MICHA: You'll have so much to tell each other, the summer won't be long enough.
(SACHA *opens a small wooden-framed triptych leaning against the wall and reads the title of one of the pictures, invisible to the audience.*)

SACHA: *Flight into Egypt* by Nicolas Poussin. (*Pause. Looks up at* MICHA.) What brought you here?

MICHA: The legal system.

SACHA: And now?

MICHA: I could leave for the Continent tomorrow, if I wanted.

SACHA: (*Holding up Dacha's apron*) Why don't you?

MICHA: Sometimes I ask myself that question when I'm in bed. The pay's good here.

SACHA: It isn't the same for my mother. She can't leave.

MICHA: Don't forget, little brother, your mother is listed as an Enemy of the People.

(ERNST *appears in the doorway.*)

ERNST: You've come! Dacha was expecting you tomorrow. Was the door open?

MICHA: Yes, doctor, the door was open.

(*He holds his cap in his hands.*)

ERNST: Wait! She'll be here.

(ERNST *disappears hurriedly.*)

SACHA: Who's he?

MICHA: He's your stepfather.

SACHA: How?

MICHA: Your mother's been with him for about seven years, I think.

SACHA: They aren't married?

MICHA: I wouldn't know, but they met in the Zone, and there aren't any wedding dresses in the Zone.

SACHA: You called him 'doctor'?

MICHA: One of the rare good ones, Uncle Ernst Moisseevitch. Uncle Permanganate we used to call him. Poor sod, he's still got five years to do.

SACHA: How's that? You say he lives here, with my mother.

MICHA: In the afternoons, Ernst Moisseevitch treats the Bruise . . .

SACHA: The Bruise?

MICHA: The Bruise are the law here. He treats some of them and their families. That way he often gets a free pass out of the Zone into the town until eleven o'clock at night. (*Pause.*) He's gone to fetch your mother now, so I'll be off.

SACHA: How did they meet there – inside?

MICHA: Don't ask me. It's rare you can get away with it. For 58s love is listed as a crime.

(*A knock at the door.* LYDIA *enters carrying a saucepan. Having*

131

put down the saucepan, she pointedly ignores MICHA *and goes straight to* SACHA.)

LYDIA: One didn't hope to see you here so soon.

SACHA: Nor did I.

LYDIA: Your mother's great day! For years she never dared to hope to see you again! All she could take with her, when she was transferred under escort, was your name . . . Sacha. Nobody could steal that from her.

(LYDIA *glances reproachfully at* MICHA. ERNST *enters, smiling. He strides across to* SACHA *still carrying his medical bag. He taps* SACHA *on the chest, a caricature of a chest examination.*)

ERNST: Fit. Congratulations. How on earth did you get here?

MICHA: I picked him up at the airport.

ERNST: You have a vehicle? (*Examines* MICHA *more closely.*) Haven't I seen you before?

MICHA: From time to time I deliver medical supplies.

ERNST: Yes, yes, a free worker. What article were you convicted under?

MICHA: Nothing special. Pickpocketing.

ERNST: Ah! An artist!

(LYDIA *starts to prepare food in the kitchen corner.* SACHA *looks a little confused.* GRICHA, *a Lenin cap on his head, an orange in his hand, enters like a whirlwind.*)

GRICHA: Our Prodigal Son has returned! Get out those trumpets, you stomping archangels! The horses are coming, the angels are marching in! Everybody outside! Line up! The Prodigal Son has returned. (*Pauses and politely shakes* MICHA'*s hand. Then, to* SACHA) Down on your knees. (SACHA *remains bewildered but self-possessed and standing.*)

Everybody down on your knees. The sweetness of the mother's breast, the authority of the father's hand on the son's head! The family home with all modern conveniences, gas, electricity, running water. Oh, the miracle of running water, hot and cold!

(DACHA *enters, taking off her scarf.* GRICHA *does not see her; his back is to the door. Nor do* LYDIA *or* ERNST. *But* SACHA, *looking over* GRICHA'*s shoulder, sees her immediately and cannot take his eyes off her.* DACHA, *as if mesmerized in her*

turn, leans against the doorpost staring back at her son.
GRICHA's *speech of welcome does not stop. The light outside is fading.*)
Long live all miracles! Never again to limp out of bed into the skimmed frozen milk of the fog. Never to be knocked over and held down by the dogs! It's finished now. Well and truly over. Long live all fairy tales! Warm yourself, little one, by the radiator. May milk and honey melt in your mouth.
(As if he has sensed the presence of DACHA, GRICHA *turns towards the door.*)
May honey melt in your mouths. Madonna and Child!
DACHA: (*Still leaning motionless against the doorpost*) Dear Gricha, let us be.
(The others busy themselves with laying the table and arranging the chairs. Mother and son, still divided by almost the entire width of the stage, watch each other, smiling. The lamp on the table is switched on. There is another knock on the door. Enter IGOR. *He bows formally to* DACHA, *as if to an audience.*)
IGOR: I was passing and I saw a light through the window . . . what a public occasion it is. Daria Petrovna! Your home is so full of people.
DACHA: (*With a gesture of her hand*) Igor Issaievitch, my son has come home.
(IGOR crosses the stage like an ambassador from DACHA *to* SACHA *and embraces him.*)
IGOR: May you always return like this, this the first time! By aeroplane or by dream, no matter the means of transport, may you always return like this.
(Everyone is moving and talking at once. We can barely distinguish their words. LYDIA *brings on a saucepan of soup.* DACHA *puts bottles on the table.* GRICHA *makes a few dance steps by himself.* MICHA *protests that he must go, and* GRICHA *insists that he stay.* ERNST *leads* SACHA *to a place at the table and everyone sits down. The chair next to* SACHA *is left vacant for* DACHA. *She is the last to sit down. She touches* SACHA's *cheek, her hand slowly descending to his chin.*)
DACHA: You've shaved.

SACHA: Yes, I shave now.

GRICHA: And supposing we drink? Red for the ladies, white for the gentlemen.

(*He pours the bottles. Hesitates before* SACHA's *glass.*)

And what will the Continent drink?

SACHA: The Continent likes vodka.

(DACHA *puts her hand over the glass to prevent* GRICHA *serving* SACHA *vodka.*)

ERNST: Let us drink to Daria Petrovna's and Sacha's happiness!

DACHA: And yours, Eric.

SACHA: And my father's!

GRICHA: To be alive at all is a sin.

(*They drink.*)

IGOR: How fine the soup is.

LYDIA: There's wild sorrel in it.

ERNST: An official order came this morning. *Convit* is no longer compulsory.

GRICHA: Everyone struggles for himself. It's obligatory.

SACHA: What is *convit*?

ERNST: A concoction made from pine needles, that everyone in the Zone is obliged to eat before the evening meal.

LYDIA: It makes you want to vomit and it takes away even the appetite of the famished. They invented it to punish us.

IGOR: Sorrel, I believe, was almost a sacred plant for the Greeks. It cured so much.

ERNST: The Academy of Medicine in Moscow has decided that whatever little good *convit* does to compensate for a lack of vitamins, it has disastrous effects on the liver. It killed thousands.

DACHA: Eat, Sachinka.

ERNST: And now we are going to be spared *convit*.

GRICHA: Ah! The perspicacity of the Academy of Medicine!

ERNST: Serebriakov, the poet, died this morning. He was reciting a verse, it was addressed to a woman called Maria. I asked him if it was an old poem. A new one, he replied.

SACHA: What did he die of?

ERNST: Alimentary dystrophy on his papers. In reality internal bleeding from the beating-up during interrogation.

LYDIA: 'They taught me the science of goodbyes in the wild sobs of the night.'

SACHA: Who?

ERNST: (*To* SACHA) Lydia Ivanovna is a specialist of our poetry in the so-called Silver Century.

(GRICHA *starts to touch* SACHA's *shirt and jacket as if he were a buyer in a shop. He takes his own cap from the back of his chair and puts it on* SACHA's *head.*)

GRICHA: The Silver Century! And our Kolyma so rich in uranium!

ERNST: (*Again to* SACHA) And Igor – Igor Issaievitch Gertzman – is a violinist. He won the First Prize in the International Concours of Vienna in 1932.

IGOR: What Ernst says, young man, is not quite true. I am no longer a violinist.

LYDIA: You will play again.

(GRICHA *imitates a violinist.*)

IGOR: Never!

SACHA: You could play if you wanted to, or don't I understand?

IGOR: How can you understand? Unless I tell you more . . .
When I was first transferred to the Zone, I had a stroke of luck. I caught typhus. Hospitalized, in quarantine, sheets, food, nurses. After the going over I'd had in Lubyanka, it was like a paradise. I could almost imagine a Stradivarius in my hands. And it was there, there in hospital, that I learned the habit of playing concerts to myself. You decide on the programme – Bach Prelude in F minor, 'Death and the Maiden', a Mozart concerto – and then you start. And with all those bars in your head, you forget the barbed wire, you forget everything else.

LYDIA: 'Of Russia's monstrous years we are the offspring . . .'

DACHA: Eat, Sacha.

ERNST: Lydia Ivanovna . . .

LYDIA: (*To* SACHA) Chief of the Planning Section for the Red October Textile Factory in Kharkov. Arrested for sabotage of the national economy.

SACHA: (*To* IGOR) So why don't you play?

IGOR: In 1939 I was transferred to a logging camp at Arkagala. There is such a silence in the *taïga*. I caught an ear infection which lead to a tympanosclerosis. But what is partial deafness for a musician? Nothing. It was the music itself which was slowly leaving my soul. It was too cold, the silence was too heavy, there was nothing inside me.

ERNST: At minus 40 Centigrade and with 400 grams of bread a day ...

IGOR: I had a friend. He slept for a while on the bunk above mine. In his other life he had been a professor of comparative religion, Professor Vassiliev. He talked to me about how he envisaged the sacred. I listened to him and I watched the fog. And then one day I suddenly heard the sense of his words and to hear this sense was like listening to another kind of music. A music that nobody can play. (*Pause.*) He had a book in English – Vassiliev – God knows how he got it. It wasn't a whole book, just part of a book, without a cover. Written by an Englishman called Fraser. I inherited this book from him along with a scarf, knitted by a woman whom Professor Vassiliev greatly loved. For the Professor died. He had great endurance and it was he who taught me my endurance. Yet he died. He died from the same disease as Serebriakov.

GRICHA: (*To* SACHA) No music there and no sense. It's pure geography.

MICHA: You're right. In the *taïga* not much sense. There's this mate of mine, he's a lorry driver too. Picked up in 'forty-seven for slaughtering his uncle's pigs. He meets a girl here in Magadan, she's a 58 in Forced Residence, like Daria Petrovna here. Liola, that's her name, and she lives in Pioneer Street. Slim, dark, with eyes like almonds, that's Liola. When he meets her, this mate of mine, she's pregnant, with no father around. So he does everything for her. Buys her a bed, buys a bath tub, buys clothes for the baby-to-be. He'd drive anywhere in the *taïga* so long as it earned him a bonus he could spend on Liola.

(SACHA *leans forward to hear this story.* LYDIA *is obviously disapproving.*)

What happens? He comes to the depot one morning and he's told to load six fucking drums of barbed wire. Where for? he asks. They tell him it's for Arkagala, where they're building a new Zone. It's a long way and there's a bloody great bonus. Transport that shit! he shouts. Never will I take that shit! We all try to reason with him. Useless. There, on the spot, the Bruise pick him up. He's back in the Zone now, this time as a 58. And where's the sense in what he did? Shouting off his big mouth?

ERNST: Perfectly correct. There's always somebody ready to unroll the barbed wire.

MICHA: I delivered it myself. Why not? And the bonus I earned, I gave it to this Liola. She was weeping her heart out for her hero. Kept on calling him her 'Decembrist'. What's that? I asked. She explained to me that it meant a Villain who changes into a hero! I look at her and think: my poor girl, where's the sense?

ERNST: Has she had her baby?

MICHA: Last month, a girl. We decided to call her Alice.

LYDIA: The water's boiling.

ERNST: Your Vassiliev, Igor, was his first name Kostia? He must be the same one. I was once in the same hut with him. He used to tell stories at night to the Villains, and they paid him with bread and protection.

IGOR: Yes, he was one of the most sought-after novelists . . . Scott, Victor Hugo, Gogol . . . He could keep twenty men quiet. Once, I remember, he refused to go on with *The Count of Monte Cristo* and, instead, he told a story which haunted me for a long time.

SACHA: Why?

IGOR: A strange story.

LYDIA: I'll serve the tea.

IGOR: When he'd finished, the Villains swore at him, and ordered him to go on with *The Count of Monte Cristo* the next night.

ERNST: Tell us the story, Igor Issaievitch.

IGOR: I've never told it before?

LYDIA: No.

137

IGOR: Once there were a people who were forgotten by the rest of the world. Perhaps they were not entirely forgotten, but they believed they were. The world fell silent, they themselves – this people – fell silent. And then one of them, a puny man who had lost most of his teeth, said: Let's go and look for the Beginning; like that, at least we'll be moving, instead of squatting here like fools. And so they set out. Quite soon they saw the walls of a city where there were great houses, palaces, temples. They said to themselves: Perhaps this city is the Beginning. As soon as they entered it, they were overcome by the stench and everywhere they stumbled over carcasses, all black and swollen. They left the city and continued on their way. Nothing got better. They crossed rivers red with blood, they crossed battlefields. They saw burned villages smoking. On and on they went, discouraged, more discouraged than when they started. Suddenly the puny man, who had lost most of his teeth, stopped and announced: We have arrived! Behind this hill is the Beginning! Behind the hill they found a small tower, broken down and useless, and a field of earth, freshly ploughed. Nothing else at all. Only one thing was strange: the sky, above the earth, didn't join the rest of the sky, it was like a separate miniature sky, set apart and on its own. So that's all there is to the Beginning! the people muttered, an acre of earth and its sky like an old hat! People need many miracles before they believe in one.

DACHA: (*Quietly*) And one miracle can make many seem possible.

IGOR: They'd had enough of travelling and forced marches and they said: We'll start again from here as if it was the Beginning. Only the puny man kept wondering about who had ploughed the earth before they came. The others set to work. They cut down the forest, they quarried, they made roads, they built towers which were useful. And as time went on, the miniature sky, above where the field had once been, grew and grew, until it was completely absorbed into the large sky. Everybody forgot about the Beginning, a regular routine set in, and nobody wondered any more about how anything began ...

(*Silence. Nobody reacts visibly to the story. We hear the clock.*
DACHA *gets up, takes the clock from the shelf and holds it up for*
ERNST *to see.*)

ERNST: I must be going. My nightly routine . . .
(ERNST *picks up his bag, strokes* SACHA's *head.* DACHA
accompanies him to the door.)

IGOR: I talk too much. It is so rare that we have a visitor from the
Continent. Forgive me, my friends. Goodnight, Sacha.
Shall I walk back home with you, Lydia Ivanovna?
(IGOR *leaves the table, accompanied by* LYDIA.)

ERNST: (*Standing by the door, addressing* IGOR *and* LYDIA) So the
two of you are leaving together for a little duet!

LYDIA: Me?

ERNST: It's never too late to begin!

MICHA: (*Getting to his feet, to* SACHA) Beyond me his story – but
Liola will understand it. I'll tell her. You know where I hang
out, if you need me.

GRICHA: (*Taking his cap*) Welcome to Magadan, Sacha. The feet
are the most intelligent part of the human body.
(*Everyone goes out of the door, saying goodbye.* SACHA *is alone.*
He sits at the table, head in hands. He visibly makes an effort,
raises his head, searches in his jacket pocket, and produces an
envelope which he places on the table. DACHA *returns and sits*
beside him.)

DACHA: Look at your plate, you've hardly eaten anything.
(*Notices the envelope.*) Where did this letter come from?

SACHA: It's for you.

DACHA: From Katya?

SACHA: (*Slowly*) No. It's from my father – or, if you like, it's
from your husband.

DACHA: (*Overwhelmed*) From Serioja!
(DACHA *takes the letter, unopened, and goes over to the window,*
standing with her back to SACHA.)
It must be an old letter.

SACHA: No. It's dated the 8th May 1952.
(DACHA *speaks to* SACHA *but with her back turned to him, in*
order to hide her face. Her voice is low as if addressed to herself.
Nevertheless she is speaking to SACHA.)

DACHA: The last news I ever had of him was at the public desk of the Cross prison on the 15th November '37. 'Transferred with no right of mail.' Those were the words. And they meant: Serioja had been executed. I'd heard the same words applied to Father in October . . . (*Turns to face* SACHA.) You must be exhausted after such a full day. *Full day!* (*Catches her breath. Walks towards him.*) You see the little room? When we knew you were coming, we built it for you.

SACHA: (*His mind elsewhere*) It wasn't necessary.

DACHA: There's a basin and a jug of water to wash your hands and face.

(*They are standing close, face to face.*)

SACHA: And my feet?

DACHA: (*With infinite tenderness*) And your feet!

(*They embrace. For an instant* SACHA's *shoulders collapse, and his head falls on to her breast. Almost immediately he straightens up and holds her at arm's length.*)

SACHA: I've come, Mama.

(SACHA *goes into his room.* DACHA *returns to the window, pensive. Lights fade.*)

Come here for a little while, Mama.

DACHA: Yes, my son, I'm coming.

(*Darkness.*)

ACT TWO

A fortnight later. Early evening. SACHA *is alone. On the table a bunch of wild flowers and a bottle of milk.* SACHA *is wearing different clothes, more in keeping with life in Magadan. He opens the window, fetches a vase of water, arranges the flowers in it, glances at himself in the mirror, combs his hair. Enter* DACHA.

DACHA: So the nightbird is at home for once!
    (*She takes off her shoes by the door and puts on slippers.*)
    A surprise today! The local radio station is going to broadcast something from our play at the infant school.
SACHA: What's it about?
DACHA: (*Laughing*) In our version the Wolf doesn't really eat the Grandmother! The Wolf meets Little Red Riding Hood and goes with her, like an escort, to Grandma's Convalescent Home.
SACHA: Does the Wolf look like the Bruise?
DACHA: Of course not.
SACHA: You surprise me! (*Holds out the vase of flowers towards her.*) Not for the Wolf and not for the Grandmother, but for you!
DACHA: (*Smiling*) Is the nightbird staying in tonight? It's days since we've seen you, Ernst and I.
SACHA: I'm nearly seventeen now! And think of the years I've lived through, not just any seventeen years – 1936 to 1952. Just think what he has seen, your son!
DACHA: We have to wait nine months, my little one, before you are seventeen.
SACHA: The Great Patriotic War, the Great Victory, the Transition from Socialism to Communism . . . I've seen more than you have.
DACHA: And you are still sixteen!
SACHA: That's a detail. When I didn't come home, you knew very well I was at Gricha's. Last night I was back by quarter to one. I walked with Ernst Moisseevitch as far as the Zone. Eight kilometres, there and back.

23

DACHA: How was it you met Ernst? He didn't come last night,
yet I wasn't worried, as I would have been once.

SACHA: The worst is over, Mother.

DACHA: How much you remind me of Serioja.

SACHA: Do I?

DACHA: You look up in the air when you're telling a story, just
like Serioja.

SACHA: Like this?

DACHA: Tell me, Sachinka, how did you meet Ernst last night?

SACHA: That's a story in itself, a Magadan story. What I like
about being here is that I meet so many people . . . and one
of the places where I meet people is the Continental.

DACHA: It's a kind of hotel.

SACHA: Hotel! You see how you need a sixteen-year-old to tell
you about Magadan!

DACHA: That I need you, yes, Sacha.

SACHA: It's a hotel for Zeks who've just got their release and who
are waiting to go to the Continent. An extraordinary place, a
real club for gentlemen, nothing like your crummy Cultural
Centre.

DACHA: There's a library at the Centre with books that are
unfindable anywhere else.

SACHA: I met a number at the Continental who speaks six
languages, and has been all round the world.

DACHA: So far?

SACHA: It's not far, it's in a little street that leads down to the
Nagaiev Bay, close to the sea, it's a basement, well-heated –
well, it's even suffocating this weather, very large. Where
else can they go, your Zeks? They can't all have super love
affairs with great doctors. So they hang out there.
Greenhorns who have just been released, others who can't
make up their minds whether to go or stay, all of them
waiting for their boat to come in – mostly they aren't in
Forced Residence, like you. It's a real museum, the
Continental. Kids, babies, women doing their washing,
cooking, singing. Little groups of men talking – talking
about really serious things. Girls too, plenty of girls with nail
varnish and even permanent waves! All this just a stone's

throw from the sea. It must be strange in the winter when the waves on the bay are frozen.

DACHA: Winter is what's normal here, it's these two months now, the months you are here, which are abnormal.

SACHA: There's a girl called Helena who has a super voice. Gypsy love songs she sings, you can't believe it. And do you know, she offered, just like that, she offered to teach me to play the guitar.

DACHA: (*Putting her hand to her forehead*) Really?

SACHA: (*Oblivious of the effect his words are having on his mother*) I've chatted with some hard cases. Tough guys. Men who really committed crimes against the State, not a question of words like most of you. Hard cases if you like, but they're not bone-headed. They think things out, they plan carefully. To hijack a cargo ship for instance. The guards are always pissed, so it would be child's play to disarm them . . .

DACHA: (*Her hand to her heart*) Stop, Sacha!

SACHA: (*Suddenly aware of his mother*) I never drink anything there, Mother, except tea, and I never go there alone. I never go there without Micha.

DACHA: And what sort of record does Micha have? There are drug-pushers, there is venereal disease, and worst of all, worse than you can ever imagine, there is the Bruise.

SACHA: I never go without Micha.

DACHA: That doesn't reassure me.

(*The light begins to dim, slowly, as the evening draws in.*)

SACHA: What have all you 58s got against Villains? They're victims like you.

DACHA: The Villains and the Bruise speak the same language.

SACHA: And that, Maman, is what I'm trying to learn something about. Yesterday I talked to a 58 – a Party Secretary of the district of Saratov. Ten years inside and they've changed absolutely nothing for him. He sits in the Continental with a red pencil, correcting the articles he reads in the *Kolyma Red Star*. And he's convinced that, since he had served his sentence for the 'regrettable error' he made in 'thirty-seven, he will now be able to continue his career in the Party and make up for lost time.

145

DACHA: (*Almost to herself*) So many lost times . . .

SACHA: If only you could meet Ignatiev! There's a hero – a man tempered like steel, as they say in school. Ignatiev was a ship's captain of a large ocean-going freighter. At the beginning of the war he was transferred to a cruiser of the Baltic Fleet. He fought the Germans off Leningrad, fought like a tiger. Only when it was hopeless did he break the German blockade and get his ship and crew safely to Sweden, where they were interned until 'forty-five. After the victory he requested to be sent home. Request accorded. The rest you can imagine. Now that he is out, he won't be had a second time! He'll get away, he has the sea in his blood, Ignatiev.

DACHA: 'Fathers can be found anywhere', that's what your father wrote to me in his letter, remember? 'My one wish,' he said, 'is that Sacha may one day rejoin you.' Be careful, Sacha!

SACHA: Don't think he's a dreamer, Ignatiev, he has it all worked out. Alaska is no distance from here. You'll see, they'll make it to America!

DACHA: When you walked with Ernst back to the Zone last night, what did you talk about?

SACHA: About God. Why do you ask? (*Looks at the clock.*) Isn't he late?

DACHA: What?

SACHA: Ernst, Maman! Look at the time.

DACHA: Don't worry. Half an hour, an hour late, is nothing. He's not always his own master. I'll put on the supper.
(*She switches on the table lamp.*)

SACHA: Can you imagine Ernst Moisseevitch as he was when he was young? When he was my age?

DACHA: Yes, easily, just as I can imagine you in twenty-five years' time . . .
(*Enter* ERNST *with his newspaper packets. He switches on the ceiling light. He looks and acts tired. He salutes* SACHA, *and then, straightaway and without a word, as in the first scene, he takes* DACHA's *blood pressure.*)

ERNST: Twenty.
(*He goes to wash his hands and takes too long about it.*)

DACHA: Don't worry, Eric.

(*They sit down.* DACHA *serves the soup.*)

SACHA: When you were my age, Ernst Moisseevitch, did you know you wanted to be a doctor?

ERNST: Yes, I did. When I was younger still, I dreamt of being a sailor.

(ERNST *sees* DACHA *taking some salt to put into her soup.*)

More salt! No, Dashinka, not in your condition.

DACHA: I've been learning things about the sea of Okhotsk this evening, Eric.

ERNST: Icebound for seven months of the year.

DACHA: It's child's play, it seems, to cross it and go to America.

ERNST: How's that?

DACHA: By boat, of course!

SACHA: Via Alaska . . .

ERNST: (*Drily*) Ah yes! I see. I never thought of that.

(*He stops eating.*)

DACHA: How was your day?

ERNST: Eventful. (*Takes off his glasses and puts them on again.*) Last night I was called to the Continental – a heart case. I gave the man an injection and who should I see but our poet here (*nods towards* SACHA) drinking tea in company. We left together and he accompanied me back to the Zone. (*Again takes off his glasses.*) When we came out of the hotel, I noticed one of the Bruises' lorries and I said to myself; a routine check up. Better, I thought, for Sacha not to be there when the Bruise arrive, you never know, but in general they turn a blind eye to most of what goes on at the Continental. I was mistaken. Do you know what happened after we left? They pulled in your entire tea party – they're inside now – Ignatiev and all his pals.

SACHA: I don't believe it! Ignatiev is too smart to get arrested for nothing!

ERNST: I suppose the ideas about the Sea of Okhotsk came from your tea party?

DACHA: (*Putting her head between her hands*) Eric, how to tell him, how to explain to him?

(SACHA *gets up and goes to stand by the window.*)

147

For a whole hour he's been telling me stories about hijackings, heroes, Alaska, escapes. Everything is like an adventure film to him. What can we do? What can we say so that they understand?

ERNST: (*Very calm*) Our lives here, Sacha, can never be a film, never. We have lost many things, things that people take for granted elsewhere. And one of the most important things we've lost is the right to be seen. Everything we live has become invisible. (*Switches on the lamp on the table.*) Even if, by some miracle, somebody made a film of our lives here in Kolyma, all that would be seen on the screen would be a blizzard, with visibility reduced to a few metres. The blizzard of our losses. Nobody would be able to see the little we've managed to protect from the blizzard. The grains on which we live are invisible. You come here. I'm not sure what a boy of your age thinks. It's a very long time ago since I was sixteen. Probably you find us colourless, a peculiar mixture of passivity and nervousness.

SACHA: That's not true!

ERNST: I'm sure you believe that somehow we can choose. Choose like Ignatiev to put to sea and cross the Bering Straits! You are wrong. Ignatiev has been arrested. Here there are no choices – or no choices like you imagine.

SACHA: You're saying none of you have any choices!

ERNST: Everything outside forbids a choice. The choices we make are inside.

(*He indicates his chest. There is a pause.* SACHA *still beside the window.* DACHA *is sewing.* ERNST *is eating his soup, spoon in one hand.*)

When you drag yourself back after a day's work in the *taïga*, when you are marched back, half dead with fatigue and hunger, you are given your ration of soup and bread. About the soup you have no choice – it has to be eaten whilst it's hot, or whilst it's at least warm. About the 400 grams of bread you have a choice. For instance, you can cut it into three little bits: one to eat now with the soup, one to suck in the mouth before going to sleep on your bunk, and the third to keep until next morning at ten, when you're working in the

taïga and the emptiness in your stomach feels like a stone.
(SACHA *moves from his place by the window and goes towards the cooking stove.* ERNST *slowly gets to his feet.* DACHA *stops sewing and watches both the men.*)
You empty a wheelbarrow full of rock. About pushing the barrow to the dump you had no choice. Now it's empty you have a choice. You can walk your barrow back just like you came, or – if you're clever, and survival makes you clever – you push it back like this, almost upright. If you choose the second way you give your shoulders a rest.
(SACHA *moves again towards the bed.* ERNST *takes the chair on which he was sitting and places it close beside* DACHA, *before sitting down on it.*)
If you are a Zek and you become a team leader, you have the choice of playing at being a screw, or of never forgetting that you are a Zek.
(*Pause.* DACHA *puts a hand on his shoulder.*)
When I receive a new contingent of the dying I have a duty to look after them all as best I can. In addition, I have the *choice* of trying to do even more, of trying to do the impossible, for one of them whom I feel must be saved at all costs.

SACHA: (*Getting up and moving towards his room*) Why not all of them?

ERNST: Because I do not have the means to choose that. (*Pause.*) Here's us, your mother and I. Since 'forty-seven when Dacha got her White Pass, she couldn't choose to leave Magadan. But she could have chosen, she can still choose, to leave me. Me, a Zek with another five years to do.

DACHA: About love there is no choice . . . and I have only one son. Tell him, Eric.

ERNST: (*Going up to* SACHA) The Continental and its gang – you understand, Sacha, all that must stop. Once and for all, you understand? You can see how your mother is. Do you want to kill her?

SACHA: (*Angry*) What do you want me to do with my time? Who do you want me to see? The kids of your Bruise officers? You want me to arse-crawl with the Bruise? Or do you want me to kick my heels here all day whilst both of you are out

149

working? Forced Residence for everyone!
(*He opens the door to his room, enters and slams it behind him.*
ERNST, *equally angry, seizes the doorhandle and pulls it
violently towards him to open it. The makeshift door comes off its
hinges. He tries to put it back. Fails.* SACHA *remains invisible.*
DACHA *comes to* ERNST'S *help. Together, solemnly, they carry
the door across the stage and lean it against the wall, near the
front door. When they turn they see* SACHA, *framed in his
doorway, wearing a sailor's cap.*)
(*Smiling*) Never mind, I don't need the door. Without a
door, we can communicate better, no?

DACHA: Your cap?

SACHA: A present from Captain Ignatiev.

DACHA: It quite suits you.

ERNST: You can't go out in a cap like that.

DACHA: (*Going up to* SACHA *and adjusting the cap on his head*) Like
this.

SACHA: (*Indicating the alarm clock*) Look at the time, Ernst
Moisseevitch. (*To* DACHA) Let's both go with him tonight.

ERNST: Not in that outfit.

SACHA: No, chief, without it.
(*He takes off the cap. All three exit. They leave the lights on.
For a moment nothing changes on the empty stage. Then the
lights begin to go down. A glass jug of water falls off the table. A
mixture of distant sounds: wind, the shouts of guards, dogs
barking. None of it is dramatic. What we hear are like the
sounds of a distant play in another theatre. A beam of light falls
on the middle of the stage. The rest in darkness. From the back
of the auditorium a man's voice mixes with the other sounds
and quickly dominates them. It is* SERIOJA'*s voice reading his
letter.*)

SERIOJA: Dacha, my little darling, how to find the words now?
Can you imagine, out of the darkness, out of the darkness of
so many years, I received a letter from Katya. Like one of
those flashes of light in Plato's cave. I learned that you are
alive, that Sacha is almost grown up. How can such miracles
happen? I have to pinch myself to make sure I'm awake.
Yes, I am. Fifteen years! For fifteen years, too, I haven't

150

held a pen, so don't be hard on my handwriting. A guard fetched me this morning, brought me here to the office, gave me this pen and paper and said: You have the right of addressing one letter to your wife. And me, idiot that I am, I started to cry. Where are you, my little one? I go back and back to the bridge in front of the Hermitage. Each paving stone, each arch of the bridge which we used to cross together, you in your black dress with a satchel – all, all is engraved. We were always in a hurry – for we had to go and fetch Sacha. I have lost my teeth and I have lost the toes of both feet. Since three years I have been on the stoves in the bath house, a merciful job for I'm no longer cold. I don't have much appetite, which is just as well. I suck with my gums and eating takes a long time. I'm not like an old man, I'm more like an old child who has forgotten his age. Hegel used to say that the difference between a dead person and a child is that the child doesn't have a memory. There our philosopher made a mistake because he couldn't foresee an intermediate category: one who is neither newborn, nor old, nor dead, nor living, yet who has a memory. I always believed that the magic of your hands wasn't in your hands but was in the way your hands obeyed your eyes. You must have said I was dead and now I come back, alive! If I'm not transferred to the mines, I'll hold out, and you must go on thinking of me as dead, you will be closer, my heart, to the reality. My soul, my spirit, my memory have long since joined those of the dead who are, after all, the majority; and, in comparison with whom, the living are rare. Try not to think of me as being here, think of me rather as one who has already joined the Spirit of History which is watching over you from the furthest stars. I know every square millimetre of your body, astonishingly and eternally. My one wish is that Sacha may one day rejoin you. Fathers can be found anywhere. Know all this, my darling. As for me, I know it, and this knowledge is like a guiding star which will show me, until my last breath, where to place my frozen feet. We are already saved!

(*Everything on the stage resumes its normal appearance. Silence.*

Enter DACHA *and* SACHA. DACHA *takes off her scarf by the door.* SACHA *notices the broken glass jug and picks up the pieces.* DACHA *looks round the room, troubled, suddenly anxious.*)

SACHA: It must have been a draught. (*Shuts the window.*) The wind is getting up over the bay.

(DACHA *wanders vaguely round the room, touching things, a plate, a chair, the glasses. Rubs a finger round the rim of a glass, holds it up to the light. Suddenly decisive, she goes to the bookshelf, chooses a book and from between its pages takes out Serioja's letter. Sits down on a chair holding the letter to her breast.* SACHA *fetches a rag to wipe up the water under the table. After using it, he rolls up the rag, and starts to kick it around like a football.*)

DACHA: Go and see Gricha tomorrow, will you? He's picked up a tin of corned beef. Lydia is knitting a scarf and mittens for him. The winter will soon be here. (*Notices that she has crumpled the letter and now smooths it out on her knees.*) The first parcel must get to Serioja before November. By a miracle I got a whole salted cod today. He'll soak it in water to get rid of the salt and he'll eat it raw . . . it's very very good . . .

(DACHA *looks up at her son. He has stopped playing football with the cloth and, as if all his energy had gone, has fallen on to his knees. He sobs.* DACHA *stands behind him, her hands on his shoulders and neck and we see her, wordlessly, calming him.*)

152

A few days later. Evening. SACHA *and* GRICHA *are sitting on two chairs, facing each other, in the middle of the room. Between them is a small table covered with a red rag. The evening lighting is not quite as usual. The small table is extra-lit, as if by a spotlight. The effect of a theatre within a theatre.* GRICHA *is wearing an artificial moustache, somewhat reminiscent of Stalin's. It is obviously attached by elastic.*

GRICHA: Are you going to confess?

SACHA: I've already said Yes.

GRICHA: In what town?

SACHA: Babylon.

GRICHA: With who?

SACHA: We were two.

GRICHA: Fucking lie. You were three.

SACHA: Not on that spree.

GRICHA: The third came from Prague.

SACHA: I'm just a bit vague.

GRICHA: Pure chicanery.

SACHA: A counter-revolution.

GRICHA: His name please!

SACHA: Diogenes.

GRICHA: Where did you meet?

SACHA: In Gorky Street.

GRICHA: This confirms what has been said.

SACHA: With how many blows to the head?

GRICHA: You scab, you sore, you blight on the people's body,
   listen to me. (*Approaches* SACHA.) When I pull on this chain,
   you stand up. When I pull a second time, you sit down.
   (*Pulls an imaginary chain, in the air by his right-hand shoulder.*)
   On to your feet!
   (SACHA *gets up.* GRICHA *pulls on the chain again.*)
   Down !
   (SACHA *sits.*)
   Stand! Sit! Stand!

(*Whilst* SACHA *is standing,* GRICHA *discreetly takes away the chair, resumes his place, pulls the chain.* SACHA *sits and falls to the floor.*)

You scabby shit – nothing, nothing will teach you! If there's no chair there, my sweet little one, you stay like this – just as if there was a chair! If I order you to sit, it means there's something to sit on! Let me see you sit.

(SACHA *sits on air, as if there was a chair there.* GRICHA *slightly corrects his posture with his hand.*)

All right, my monkey, you stay like that. Twenty-four hours on that chair and ideas will come to you by the hundred.

(GRICHA *sits down at his place behind the table.* SACHA *is sitting on air.*)

Now – I want the names of your accomplices.

SACHA: Come plis this way, come plis!

GRICHA: (*Furious, pulling the chain continuously*) Up! Down! Up! Down! Why did Diogenes offer you gum to chew?

SACHA: That's not true.

GRICHA: Shit! Do you think you can reply like that, you! The only negative reply we permit is: 'Not in my presence.'

SACHA: Not in my presence!

GRICHA: (*Standing up in his fury*) Do you want the ice bin?

SACHA: Frédéric Chopin.

GRICHA: At last a name!

SACHA: Do you prefer Schumann?

GRICHA: Schumann, Haussemann, Huissman! So you were seven.

SACHA: Yes, seven with Sunday.

GRICHA: That's better, you're learning how to play.

SACHA: We met on Fridays.

GRICHA: Traitors – (*Pretends to think.*) – Babylon – Prague – Diogenes – chewing gum – America – Chopin, Frédéric – the Bering Sea – Alaska – a conspiracy against the Cheka!

(*From under the table he picks up a raw herring and begins to slap* SACHA's *face with it.* SACHA, *sitting on air, remains immobile.*)

Fascist! Organist! Archivist! Nationalist! Continental Tourist!

(*A knock at the door.* SACHA *stands up.* GRICHA *rips off his moustache, and stuffs it into his pocket. His haste indicates nervousness. He grabs the red cloth off the table and throws it under the bed.*)
Come in.
(*Enter* MICHA. *Not as we have seen him before. Pale, slovenly. He sits down on the chair where* SACHA *sat.*)
(*To* MICHA) You look as though you've had a real going over, my boy. Sacha, do we have anything in the First Aid Kit?
(*Silence.* SACHA *brings over two glasses and a bottle of unlabelled alcohol.*)
Neat or with water?

MICHA: Neat.
(GRICHA *pours out.* SACHA *fetches a plate of gherkins.* MICHA *takes a gherkin and knocks back his glass.*)
Where's your mum and dad?

SACHA: They've gone to the film of the week. Vivien Leigh and Robert Taylor, what is it called?

MICHA: You should have heard the dressing down your old man gave me the other day. About taking you to the Continental. It was like the wrath of God.

SACHA: I saw you yesterday on Stalin Avenue. You looked like somebody in a trance.

MICHA: They've picked up Liola.

SACHA: Arrested?

MICHA: Nicked.

GRICHA: Which Liola? Who is she?

SACHA: Liola – you don't remember? The girl of his mate, the lorry-driver, the girl who was pregnant. A 58 with almond-shaped eyes. The lorry-driver got arrested for talking out loud, and Liola was very proud of him. He was her Decembrist, she said.

GRICHA: (*Very precise*) When was she arrested, this Liola?

MICHA: They picked her up last night, at her place. She was feeding the infant. Alice. She called her baby Alice.

GRICHA: Yes. Yes. I see. So Liola has gone to join her Decembrist – as the poets used to say. How out of date these poets are today! Nobody joins anybody in the Zone.

155

MICHA: (*Quietly*) I'm going to wait for her.

GRICHA: Her? Who?

MICHA: Liola.

> (GRICHA *fills up the two glasses. Hands one to* MICHA *and one to* SACHA.)

No, no, not for Sacha. Ernst Moisseevitch would kill me.

SACHA: (*Winking at* GRICHA *who drinks the glass in question*) Never in my presence! I don't understand, Micha. I just don't understand. Is it your mate or is it you who loves this Liola with almond eyes?

MICHA: Ten years, twenty years – I'm going to stay here in Kolyma and wait for her.

GRICHA: (*Sarcastically*) And you'll send her little parcels!

SACHA: Why not? We sent a parcel to Father today.

GRICHA: When your Liola comes out, she'll be a toothless old lady – supposing all goes well, and she behaves herself! And her Decembrist? What are we going to do about him?

MICHA: That's her business.

GRICHA: Who on earth is this Liola? A simple Villain becomes a knight in shining armour, under her spell.

SACHA: Who do you mean?

GRICHA: I'm talking about her Decembrist. And as for our poor Micha here – he was an honest thief and he's being transformed into a Don Quixote! All this for a pair of almond eyes. Ah Kolyma, Kolyma, land of paradise! If I was in your shoes, Micha, I'd have got the hell out of here long ago. I'd be in the south sun-bathing. You're not condemned like us to stay here for life, and you're young.

MICHA: Liola isn't the only one. They are picking up others too. There's a rumour they're going to arrest all the 58s for the second time.

GRICHA: (*Softly*) The third time for me. (*Pause.*) Your victim with the almond eyes – tell me – what's her name?

MICHA: Liola.

GRICHA: Liola *what*, for heaven's sake? Tell me her surname!

MICHA: Annissimov.

GRICHA: And the others they've arrested, do you know their names?

MICHA: No, I don't think so, let me think. In any case, what does it matter, if you don't know them? Hang on, yes, there's this bloke – he's lost an arm – lives just down the street from us, they arrested him this morning, and his name is Avevtchenko.

SACHA: What's happened to Liola's baby daughter? Alice, you said.

MICHA: She's been bundled off into an orphanage – the special one for the kids of the Enemies of the People.

GRICHA: Annissimov . . . Avevtchenko . . . Alice.

(*A knock on the door. Enter* LYDIA *and* IGOR. LYDIA *wears a smartish dress with a fox fur round her shoulders.* IGOR *has a white scarf over his usual jacket. As they enter* MICHA *gets up to leave.*)

IGOR: We were passing and we saw a light in the window . . .

SACHA: Come and sit down, make yourselves at home.

MICHA: I'm off . . . I have some mates waiting. (*To* SACHA) I really came to ask you something. Next week I'm doing a trip into the *taïga*. Supplies for a group of geologists working in the north, I've been there once, and they're mostly from Moscow. Come with me if you can, it'll be company.

SACHA: Is it far?

MICHA: About two hundred by road, and then a hundred cross-country.

SACHA: I'd like to come but you know how it is. I must ask Ernst Moisseevitch first. If he says yes, I'll come. Something else I thought of. Mother has a friend who works in the orphanage. Perhaps she could arrange for you to go and see Alice if you wanted to . . .

(MICHA *nods and exits without a word.*)

LYDIA: He looked as if he was in trouble, your criminal friend there, what is it?

GRICHA: Nothing, nothing at all.

IGOR: And you two, you look like conspirators of some sort. What's been going on here?

SACHA: Just an evening's theatre.

LYDIA: And do you know what we did tonight? We went to see a film. A real English melodrama, set in London of all places!

SACHA: Yes, with Vivien Leigh and Robert Taylor. My parents are there now.

LYDIA: We went to the earlier programme.

IGOR: Daria Petrovna and Ernst Moisseevitch will enjoy themselves. It's about a man who comes back from the war, wounded. His hair has gone white. The woman who was the great love of his life believes that he is dead. And in her grief and desperation, she has become – a fallen woman.

SACHA: Do you know, Igor Issaievitch, nowadays, such a woman is called a tart!

IGOR: One day they meet again and that's where the story begins. She is very beautiful, and he is an aristocrat. If I understood correctly. The strangest thing of all was that everybody at the Cultural Centre, sitting there in the dark, everybody was wiping their eyes and snivelling. The Bruise with their wives and children, and we who were once Zeks – and will probably be Zeks again – masters and slaves, we all reacted in the same way to this love story . . . there's a waltz in the film which is like a refrain. (*Hums it.*) My mother used to play the very same waltz at home when she gave dancing lessons. I can still see her fingers, very long and white, flying over the yellow keys of our piano, which was far from new, and her head bent forward and her fair hair rather untidy . . . The timbre of that piano was wonderful, a little dry, cold, metallic, just what I liked from a piano.

(*He hums the waltz again, louder than before.*)

GRICHA: Keep it up, Igor Issaievitch, keep it up! The moment has come for you to learn to dance a waltz, Sacha!

(*He pulls* SACHA *to the middle of the room and demonstrates the steps.*)

One . . . two . . . three – don't walk on my feet – one . . . two . . . three . . . you see . . . it's simple, simpler than an interrogation . . . one . . . two . . . three.

(*He makes* SACHA *turn faster.*)

You are gifted, my prince, that has to be said. One . . . two . . . three . . . you are gifted.

(LYDIA *takes* IGOR *by the hand and leads him to dance. All four dance and hum the tune.*)

158

LYDIA: (*To* IGOR) You haven't forgotten . . . you haven't forgotten anything.
(*She closes her eyes. A recording of their humming, with a piano added, now takes over as music.*)

IGOR: The waltz, with its unique rhythm, was, you know, an invention of the nineteenth century. According to Spengler, the tempo of the waltz corresponds exactly to the spirit of modern man . . . the same steps repeated but always at a new level . . . a kind of diagram in dance of the Hegelian dialectic.
(*He shuts his eyes and the two of them dance intensely.*)

GRICHA: Your son-of-a-bitch Hegelian dialectic has cost us something, and it's not over yet. To hell with your dialectic! And to hell with its mother and father!
(*The four dance with more and more verve, then slow down.*)

IGOR: No need to have it in for Hegel. If Marx hadn't taken his dialectic and turned it on its head . . .

GRICHA: We wouldn't all be here and Magadan wouldn't . . .
(*SACHA accelerates their movement so that* GRICHA *is forced to stop talking.*)

IGOR: (*Softly*) Surely we wouldn't be here.
(*The four are still dancing.*)

SACHA: You say Marx stood it on its head, but didn't he stand it on its feet? And that's how the dialectic became materialist . . . one . . . two . . . dialectical materialism.

LYDIA: (*Clinging very close to* IGOR) Sacha is right, what he says rings a bell. But before we were dancing so well . . . with or without a dialectic!
(*Out of breath,* LYDIA *stops and leads* IGOR *to the table. The music continues.*)
(*To the others*) We are going to give violin lessons.

IGOR: (*Drily and a little breathlessly*) Don't start again, I beg you, Lydia Ivanovna. It's out of the question. Music in all its forms is over for me, do you understand? Over, once and for all. And where I am now, in my little caretaker's room, with my notebooks and my little library, I am happy there. I earn a living and I have no boots to lick. I sweep the cinema, I pile up chairs, I regulate the radiators . . .

LYDIA: The lessons would only be for children.

IGOR: *Their* children.

(GRICHA *and* SACHA *are still dancing but* GRICHA *is out of breath.*)

GRICHA: Don't be so pig-headed, Igor, each of us has to live.

IGOR: I do live, thank you.

LYDIA: You live, you think you live! Your room is damp. You have how many broken ribs? You have rheumatism, Igorik! My room is sunny and twice as big. In your basement there's not even room for a double bed.

IGOR: My bed is still a bed, incomparably preferable to a bunk in the Zone.

(GRICHA *and* SACHA *have stopped dancing and the music dies away.* GRICHA *sits down.*)

GRICHA: It sounds like a family quarrel! Ah! How beautiful they were, those family quarrels!

SACHA: (*Sitting on one of the chairs of the 'Interrogation' scene in the middle of the room*) It's true, Igor Issaievitch, her room, the room of Lydia Ivanovna is better.

GRICHA: And what a good cook she is! What a housekeeper!

LYDIA: Will you all shut up please? We can settle this ourselves.

IGOR: (*Very gently and softly*) My bed is not a bunk.

GRICHA: Perhaps you ought to settle your affairs quickly.

LYDIA: Rumours, rumours, they're all we have to go by here. Yes, yes. There have been a few isolated arrests, I'm fully aware of that. But I have heard, and I have it from the highest authority, that a new wave of arrests is out of the question, there are going to be no mass arrests.

SACHA: Mass arrests. What does that mean? How many make a mass? How many Zeks are there on the planet of Kolyma?

LYDIA: Many thousands.

IGOR: A mathematician I knew in the Zone – who was an expert in statistics in his first life – made his own calculations about the population of our planet. For a while he worked as a clerk in the administration. According to him it was between 3 and 4 million.

LYDIA: (*Lowering her voice*) Igor, please, it's better not to be heard quoting numbers.

IGOR: No statistics and no music lessons!

160

(A long silence. Sound of the clock.)

SACHA: He's going to die, he's not immortal and then life will change.

LYDIA: *(Frightened)* What on earth is the child saying? From where did you get such ideas?

SACHA: From here of course. From you. Everyone here knows very well that everyone has got to die. On the Continent they are so scared they believe he may be an exception.

(GRICHA paces round the room like an animal in a small cage.)

IGOR: What he says is not stupid, not stupid at all. May heaven protect you, Sacha. We must be going now. It has done me a lot of good to see you, Sacha. Perhaps somebody like you can bear witness. It's very important for us to have a witness. And you are right – he's not immortal, with his arteries thickening with so much blood – not *his* blood needless to say – the blood of others. But maybe it comes to the same thing – phhh!

SACHA: What's more, he's old. Seventy-two.

GRICHA: *(Suddenly stops pacing)* Power is an aphrodisiac. Georgians live a long time – with their mountains and their yoghurts and red peppers . . .

LYDIA: It's late, late, we really must be going.

(IGOR, lost in his thoughts, does not stir.)

Igor Issaievitch, there will be all the chairs to stack after the film.

(He still does not move. LYDIA takes his hand gently.)

Igorik, come on, dear.

IGOR: Yes, I'm coming.

(IGOR starts to hum the waltz. The two of them leave. SACHA and GRICHA sit down on the same two chairs as at the beginning of the scene. The small table between them.)

GRICHA: Annissimov – Avevtchenko – Alice, yes, Alice is a Christian name. Still, you can see the logic. Annissimov – Avevtchenko – the cunning bastards.

(GRICHA takes the moustache out of his pocket. SACHA fetches a box of matches from the stove, strikes one, and leans across the table with the idea of setting fire to the moustache. GRICHA blows out the match.)

You – you understand nothing! You are just a tourist here! Nothing more than a tourist.

(*He begins to pull the imaginary chain, but this time it is he himself who stands up and sits down. His voice is no longer playful, but violent, bordering on hysteria.*)

Up! Down! Up! There's no end to it, it goes on and on, everything starts again, when it is over, it starts again at the beginning – be–ginn–ing, be–ginn–ing. (*Shouting but, by force of habit, prudently so that he cannot be heard in the street*) The in–ex–or–ab–le hell of ge–og–ra–phy.

ACT THREE

About a fortnight later. Evening. The days are getting shorter. It is nearly September. ERNST, DACHA, SACHA, *sitting at the table are in the middle of a conversation.*

SACHA: ... when I was there, I understood better what Igor Issaievitch was saying about the silence. And I understood something about myself, about my fears. Can you get rid of fears? I don't think so. You have to make a place for them, and then keep them in their place. It's normal to be frightened, isn't it? What's dangerous is when fears break free, then there's panic. It's as if you have to make a room for every one of your fears ... with a window and a door.

DACHA: Yes ... yes ... yes.

ERNST: What did they talk about, your geologists?

SACHA: About the Cenozoic era which lasted seventy million years. They were palaeontologists, Ernst Moisseevitch. And do you know what they had just discovered? A mammoth – a giant mammoth in perfect condition. He looked as if he were alive yesterday, fresh as a daisy. I brought back a present for you.

(SACHA *fetches a parcel from his room.* ERNST *and* DACHA *exchange amused glances.*)

(*Holding out the parcel to* ERNST) It's for you.

ERNST: (*Taking it and then giving it to* DACHA) Really for me?

DACHA: (*Carefully unwrapping the paper and the cotton-wool*) What on earth is it?

(*She holds the object up.*)

SACHA: A mammoth's tooth!

DACHA: It isn't, I can't believe it!

(*She holds it out at arm's length, near* ERNST's *mouth.*)

Smile, Ernst! Smile and show us your teeth!

(ERNST *gives an enormous grin. Everyone laughs.*)

ERNST: Did you know mammoths used their tusks as snow ploughs? They were well adapted to their habitat.

DACHA: Smile, mammoth! Show us all your teeth!

ERNST: (*Smiling*) By the way, there's no more toothpaste – not even in *their* shop. Deliveries have stopped. (*To* SACHA) Try to send us some from Leningrad. (*Takes out of his pocket a bundle of bank notes tied up with a piece of string.*) This is the money for your ticket. At the latest you should get it for next Friday.

DACHA: Almost a week.

ERNST: That way you'll be there for the beginning of term, and have time to sort out your books. And don't forget to send a telegram to your aunt tomorrow, as soon as you know the time of your plane.

DACHA: From the house to the school is just two tram stops, isn't it?

SACHA: When it's fine, I walk.

ERNST: Micha will find the means to get you to the airport. The weather forecasts are good. They're not predicting the fog till the end of September this year. The planes won't be grounded. You'll easily get a place, but be good and book it tomorrow.
(SACHA *goes back into his room and returns with a long-handled broom – as is used for sweeping streets.*)

DACHA: (*Laughing*) And what's this magic? We've got a broom, Sacha, you know that.

SACHA: The palaeontologists had ten brooms like this! An administrative error! So they gave me one.
(ERNST *has been checking the money and is now retying the string around the wad of notes.*)

ERNST: For brushing the mammoth's teeth, perhaps, Sacha? . . . When I was a child there was a toothpaste which smelt of cucumbers. Pale green in colour. Odd how your broom brings that back to me. No – not so much – it was the gardener sweeping the leaves, he had a broom which seemed to me to be as tall as a tree . . . Perhaps on the Continent they still produce a toothpaste that smells a little artificially of cucumbers?

SACHA: (*Preoccupied*) Maybe . . .

(DACHA *fetches the triptych, places it on the table, opens it – its back to the audience.*)

DACHA: Will you do something for me, Sachinka? One day when you have time, walk across the bridge and go and look at these three pictures in the Hermitage. Look at them for yourself – and for us. When I got my White Pass and I found this room for us to live in, in the way you have seen, and the way we have to live, well, it was then that I found these three reproductions, and they were the first present, real present, which I ever gave to Ernst.

(SACHA *looks carefully at the images, then shuts the triptych.*)

SACHA: I'm not going back to Leningrad. Not for the Hermitage. Not for some toothpaste.

ERNST: You have to be serious, Sacha.

SACHA: I'm staying here.

ERNST: Sacha, arguments are not good for your mother's blood pressure . . .

DACHA: Please, Sacha.

SACHA: I'm staying.

ERNST: Let us examine the situation carefully. You've spent your holidays here, you've seen a lot – even a mammoth! You have found your mother after fifteen years . . .

DACHA: We'll see each other again soon, we'll spend many, many, many days together.

ERNST: You can come back next year.

SACHA: When?

ERNST: The 4th of July 1953!

DACHA: You'll have finished school by then, we'll have plenty of time to talk, to talk about your future.

SACHA: What future?

ERNST: We'll be able to discuss, you'll be able to talk with us, about what you want to do with your life.

SACHA: (*Calmly*) What I am – whether I want it or not – has already been decided, once and for all, by my mother and father.

(*Silence.* DACHA, *visibly troubled, goes to the 'kitchen corner' by the sink.*)

167

ERNST: (*Speaking precisely but with much hesitation*) If what you mean, if what you have just said means that Dacha, your mother, and Serioja, your father, both of them belonging to the population of Zeks, if what you mean is that you, as their son, risk, as a consequence of being their son, to be marked for life, you are partly right, and we must admit it, but only partly right. Only partly right, Sacha, because I believe that a man's life is not really determined by the accident of his birth in a particular place during a particular year to two particular parents – all these particulars are what *they* note in their files – this counts for a lot, but everything I have seen leads me to believe that the accident of birth is not what finally counts.

DACHA: We have so few choices and, day after day, we choose. Is it a different way of choosing?

ERNST: Each one of us comes into the world with her or his unique possibility – which is like an aim, or, if you wish, almost like a law. The job of our lives is to become – day by day, year by year, more conscious of this aim so that it can at last be realized. If we want to, we can know it. Magadan and Leningrad – geography and history, parents and occupation, it's all accidental. A question of chance. But to beat the accidental, Sacha, is to respect the law and to achieve the aim.

SACHA: And in what paragraph is your wonderful law inscribed?

ERNST: (*Smiling*) The unfindable one. (*Pause.*) It's inscribed differently in each one of us – inscribed by God at the same moment as he gave us life . . .

(*Enter* GRICHA, *downcast as we have never seen him. He takes a chair at the table.*)

DACHA: Some tea?

(GRICHA *shakes his head.*)

What's the matter with you?

GRICHA: Fucked up. I can't sleep. Can't sleep a wink. I just lie on my back thinking. I don't want to be tactless, last thing I want to do – but I've discovered something which concerns us all . . .

(*The door is flung open and a* YOUNG WOMAN *rushes in.*

168

Apparently drunk. Dishevelled hair. Unknown to anyone
present. Her voice is high and excited. Her words are slow at
first.)

YOUNG WOMAN: Can someone help me? Please someone. They
told me there might be a doctor here. Is there? Is there a
doctor in the house? You see, they laugh!
(*She comes towards the table like a blind person.* DACHA *and*
ERNST *get to their feet.*)

ERNST: I'm a doctor. What is it you're complaining of?

YOUNG WOMAN: (*Faster*) Where have they taken him, tell me,
doctor, where? Can't you, doctor, can't you give me back my
life? He's disappeared, gone, and his shoes are still under the
bed. Where have they put his feet, doctor? . . . A full bottle
of red rose-hips for his birthday. I poured out glasses for him
and for me, and I drank for him and for me. It was going to
be his birthday today. How many steps? Thirty-eight? He'll
never be late now. Now he'll never be early. And I can't go
to the port bar to bring him home. On my two feet, alone, I
can't keep going, for how long, doctor?
(DACHA *places a chair behind the* YOUNG WOMAN *and makes*
her sit. DACHA *herself stays standing behind the chair, and*
motions with her head so that ERNST *sits down where he was*
before. NB When DACHA *begins to calm the* YOUNG WOMAN,
DACHA's *face will not be directly visible to the audience.*)
It would be easier with one foot, wouldn't it? It would be
over sooner. When he came home, we drank a glass each and
we had four feet. He said: Forget it, forget it, hushaby, I
love your freckles, and I said: I want a child . . . that'll make
six feet. Do you know, doctor, how deep it is between the
double windows? One foot. I look for him there, between the
windows.
(DACHA *places her hands gently on the* YOUNG WOMAN's
back.)
He has a habit of scratching his right ear with his left hand.
(*Imitates the gesture.*) If you see him, doctor, you'll recognize
him. Tell him I've got a squirrel for him, no, two, two. How
do they cut off their own hands? How do they open their
own veins? (*Begins to become calmer.*) Don't think about it,

he told me, have a drink and forget it, hushaby. Yes, yes. Don't think, no. They've taken him, yes. They've broken my heart, yes. (*Almost calm*) It is so so hard to say yes. (*She leans her head back against* DACHA's *breast.*) To what office should I go with a pain like mine to get its papers? (*Pause.*) If I find a squirrel, I'll kill it. Two squirrels I'm going to kill, to make him a chapka. (*Gets up and walks steadily towards the door.*) He lost his chapka last spring. Yes, yes, he must have a chapka, yes. To keep warm, you should know that, you need two squirrels. (*She is just about to leave. No one has moved.*)

GRICHA: His name please?

YOUNG WOMAN: The same as mine. (*Exit* YOUNG WOMAN. DACHA, *visibly exhausted, grasps the back of the chair on which the* YOUNG WOMAN *was sitting.* ERNST *and* SACHA *lead her to the bed where she sits down.* ERNST *puts his arm round her shoulders and sits beside her. The corner where the bed is is only half lit.* SACHA *returns to the table where* GRICHA *is still sitting.*)

GRICHA: Forget it! Forget it! It's not bad advice. Soon it'll be our turn. I know what's happening, I know everything now. Once, the first time, at the beginning, they accused us, they brought a case against each one of us, they forced us to confess, there was a prosecution. This time it's much simpler, as simple as the ABC. They need labour and they're not getting enough from the Continent, and so they're taking us back inside, and it doesn't matter what Article we were arrested under. This time it's by alphabetical order. Last week it was the As, this week it's the Bs, it's as simple as the ABC . . . A . . . B . . . C.

DACHA: Poor kid! (*Nods towards the door.*) It's already an eternity.

GRICHA: Next week it will be the Cs, then the Ds . . . Between their alphabetical order and their geography they have us well and truly fucked.

SACHA: Sshhh . . .

GRICHA: (*Getting to his feet*) As for you, Sachinka, listen to your

170

old friend for once. Get the hell out of here, as soon as you can make it. It'll be one worry less for your mother.

SACHA: There are three people living on this planet whom I really care about. They're my world, and they are here.

(GRICHA *leaves almost on tiptoe.* ERNST *and* DACHA *are still on the bed.* SACHA, *very quietly, goes to where the door of his room is leaning against the wall, picks it up, carries it to the door frame and lowers it on to its hinges.*)

DACHA: What is it you're doing, Sacha?

SACHA: I'm staying here!

(*The door is on its hinges.*)

And if you want to get rid of me, you'll have to carry me out tied to my door!

(*Immobility. Then* ERNST *takes* DACHA *by the hand and leads her to the middle of the stage where she sits down on the chair left by the* YOUNG WOMAN. *She faces the audience.* ERNST *stands formally behind the chair and* SACHA *joins them. They pose, stiffly, as for a family photograph. Artificial lighting emphasizes this effect. Perhaps there should be a 'flash'.*)

SERIOJA: (*Voice reading from his letter, from back of auditorium*) 'He didn't foresee a third category: somebody who is neither newborn, nor old, neither living nor dead . . . but who has a memory.'

SACHA: (*Impersonal voice, no gestures or movement*) I know every square millimetre of your body, astonishingly and eternally.

ERNST: (*Straight to audience, without gestures*) You had pneumonia when you arrived. You were just one among all the other feverish and exhausted bodies. One more. So many arrivals and departures, and many of those departing were leaving on the longest journey. Some get better, others don't, and the difference between them is so slight. You, you slept all the time, Dachenka. I had four hours' sleep a night. Little by little you slept less. And when you could get out of bed, you worked as my nurse. Once I said to you: If all nurses were like you . . . and you laughed and replied: I was born under the sign of Pisces. In the woman's ward of the hospital of Camp number 102, you slept in the bed against the wall by the door, and my bed was just on the other side of

171

the wall. One night, you made your way out of the ward, and you came to me, your hands smelling of hay and honey. It was the winter of 'forty-four.

DACHA: (*Immobile*) No, Eric, it was already the month of April 'forty-four. Even with the snow, the air smelt of spring.

Two or three days later. Evening light outside. DACHA *is wearing her smart dress (as at Sacha's arrival) and high-heeled shoes. She is ironing. Beside her on the table two piles of clothes already ironed.* SACHA *is lying on his stomach on her bed. Whilst reading he cracks hazelnuts with his teeth, and eats them. The curtain rises on silence – except for the noise of the nuts and the vague sounds of the town through the window.*

DACHA: Katya's expecting you any day. Read her letter.
    (*She leaves the table and places the letter on the book* SACHA *is reading.*)
    Perhaps it's just as well you haven't told her yet.
SACHA: (*Absorbed by what he is reading*) Later . . .
    (DACHA *continues ironing.*)
DACHA: You shouldn't break the nuts with your teeth.
SACHA: Do you want me to break them with your teeth?
DACHA: Find a stone.
SACHA: Takes too long. Why don't you let me read?
DACHA: When you see Katya, please tell her about Ernst.
SACHA: Why do you go on? I've never seen anyone so pigheaded.
    The two of you, you and Ernst, you make a real pair.
    Leningrad is over, finished. Do you see? .
    (*Silence.* DACHA *arranges what she has ironed on the shelves in the cupboard.*)
DACHA: Look, Sachinka, you have to look now – here on this side are your things.
    (SACHA *continues to read.*)
    Do you want to make me angry? Listen for once!
    (SACHA *looks up.*)
    Here are Ernst's things – here are yours. Sheets and pillowcases are on the top shelf.
SACHA: Why do you tell me all that? I know it.
    (*He starts to read again.*)
DACHA: Ernst can't tell the difference between a clean shirt and a dirty one.

SACHA: For others yes, for himself, no.

DACHA: He's like a baby. You must explain to him. (*Searches in the cupboard.*) Where in God's name have I hidden my winter boots? Where? (*Takes out a dress on a coat-hanger and hangs it on top of the open cupboard door.*) This dress could do with an iron.

(She takes a pile of clothes from the cupboard and puts them on the table. She still hasn't found her boots. Kneeling on the floor, she pulls out a suitcase from under the bed on which SACHA is lying.)

Where for heaven's sake?

SACHA: What's it you're looking for?

DACHA: My winter boots.

SACHA: We're only at the end of the month of August and she's looking for her winter boots!

DACHA: They need repairing and Ernst has found a man who can do it. If he takes them tonight, they'll be ready in ten days. (*Two sharp knocks on the door. SACHA sits up. DACHA still on her knees, buries her head in her son's lap. For an instant.*) Who is it?

(DACHA gets to her feet, opens the door. Enter two BRUISE. SACHA standing by the door of his room. BRUISE I hands DACHA a blue paper – she glances at it.)

BRUISE I: It's for a routine check-up.

DACHA: (*Giving back the paper*) It was always just for a check-up. (*Smiling*) No?

(BRUISE 2 goes to the open cupboard and searches between the clothes, throwing some on the floor. He finds the wad of bank notes tied with string.)

BRUISE 2: (*Throwing the packet on the table at which BRUISE I is already seated*) And this – what is it?

DACHA: (*In the middle of the room, standing, calm*) Some money. In fact, the money for my son's return ticket to Leningrad – I applied for, and received the authorization for him to spend his school holidays here. He's leaving in a few days.

BRUISE 2: We'll see.

(BRUISE I examines the wad of money which his colleague has thrown on the table. BRUISE 2, having finished with the

174

cupboard, now goes to the bookshelf and finds the letter from
Serioja. During the search, when nothing is being said, we hear
the mechanism of the alarm clock.)

(*Throwing the letter on the table*) And this document, what is it?

DACHA: A letter from my husband – postmarked Vorkouta.

BRUISE 1: (*Examining the letter*) It seems then that you have two
husbands.

DACHA: I don't understand.

BRUISE 1: It's clear enough. You have one husband here and
another in Vorkouta.

(BRUISE 2 *picks up the triptych and puts it on the table.* BRUISE
1 *opens it and they both look at it together.*)

BRUISE 2: A religious object, used for worship. Are you a
Baptist?

DACHA: Baptist! Why on earth should I be a Baptist any more
than you?

BRUISE 1: You believe in God.

DACHA: I don't see the connection.

BRUISE 2: It's with this thing here that you say your prayers!

DACHA: Prayers? Why prayers?

BRUISE 1: Then explain what you use it for!

DACHA: (*Calm, approaching the table and standing behind the*
BRUISE, *speaking with the slow intonation of a museum guide*)
On your left, you see a Madonna by Leonardo da Vinci, the
so-called *Litta Madonna*, fifteenth century; in the middle you
can see *The Flight into Egypt* by Nicolas Poussin,
seventeenth century, French school; on your right you find
David's Farewell to Jonathan, painted by Rembrandt,
seventeenth century, Dutch. Some historians maintain that
it represents David's reconciliation with Absalom, the
gesture of David does perhaps suggest a reconciliation rather
than a farewell. All three pictures are to be found in the
Hermitage Museum in Leningrad.

BRUISE 2: We're confiscating it.

(*He looks at his colleague for approval.*)

DACHA: No! You have no right.

BRUISE 1: How did you come by these treasures? Were they
stolen?

175

SACHA: It was me. I brought these pictures from Leningrad for my mother.

BRUISE I: Did you buy them? How much did you pay for them?

SACHA: I tore them out of the art magazine *Iskustvo*. If you look carefully, you'll see they're cheap reproductions.

BRUISE 2: (*Peering close into the triptych*) They're icons and disgusting ones! Look. Look at her. Her tits are outside.

DACHA: Even you probably fed at your mother's breast.

BRUISE I: (*Folding and unfolding the wooden triptych*) You're all the same, all of you 58s. You think you're clever. But I wasn't born yesterday either. This object smells of priests. (*Turns round to address* SACHA) As for you, citizen, you'd better leave without another word.

DACHA: Please give me just five minutes. In five minutes I'll be ready, there's no need for anger, nobody is tricking you, nobody is trying to get the better of you. My son is leaving in a few days, and I'll be leaving in five minutes with you. (*Holds out her arms towards them.*) You can be sure, I am ready, everything is ready, there's no need for anything more.

(*Her arms still extended, her hands rest very lightly on the shoulders of* BRUISE I. *He rises to his feet slowly and both* BRUISE, *almost in slow-motion, move towards the open door where they wait, leaning against the door frame.* DACHA *lays out a large scarf on the table, throws her clothes into it, makes a bundle, ties a knot, and approaches* SACHA.)

Beneath so many closed eyes the sleep of no one.

(*She stuffs the wad of money into his pocket.*)

Take the plane, my boy, from the airport of Magadan. And never forget: it isn't over.

(*She goes to the door, changes into her outdoor shoes and whispers beside the two* BRUISE.)

It isn't over. It's not finished. It's not the end.

(DACHA *leaves, without turning back to look at* SACHA. *The two* BRUISE *shut the door behind them.* SACHA *alone, leaning against the partition wall of his room. We hear the clock. He does not move. Slowly he looks round the room, surveying the disorder. He wipes the back of his hand across his forehead, then he touches both of his thighs. He walks somewhat unsteadily towards the table.*)

SACHA: (*Picking up his father's letter, reinserting it into a book*) And the money, where's it gone? (*Looks on the floor.*) They left it on the table. (*Puts the triptych back into its place.*) Where could it have gone?

(*The corner of the suitcase under the bed catches his eye, he pulls it out, looks inside, holds up something wrapped in newspaper.*) The boots she was looking for!

(*A boot in each hand, he hesitates, then places them deliberately on the table and goes back to kick the suitcase under the bed. He begins to tidy the wardrobe cupboard. The lights go down.*) Bastards! 'On this side are your things. Here are Ernst's things.'

(*He continues to tidy and to pick up things from the floor. Lights very low.*)

'Sheets and pillowcases are on the top shelf. You must explain to him. He can't tell the difference between a clean shirt and a dirty one. You must explain to him. He's like a baby.'

(*Silence. Mechanism of the clock. The noise of a key in the door. Suddenly the lights are switched on by* ERNST *who stands in the doorway.*)

ERNST: (*Shouting*) Dacha! Where is Dacha?

(*He approaches* SACHA *by the wardrobe, who, head bowed, says nothing.* ERNST *puts his doctor's bag on the table; from his string bag he takes out a loaf of bread and some potatoes. Then he repeats in a whisper*) Where is Dacha?

SACHA: They came to get her.

ERNST: When?

SACHA: (*Looking at the clock*) An hour ago.

ERNST: How many were they?

SACHA: Two.

ERNST: Did they have a warrant?

SACHA: Yes, a blue bit of paper.

ERNST: What did they ask about?

SACHA: The triptych.

ERNST: Nothing else?

SACHA: Father's letter – they found it.

ERNST: Only that?

SACHA: The money. (*Feels in his pockets, finds the wad of notes.*) What a fool. It was there all the time.

ERNST: Keep the money. What did she take with her?

SACHA: What she had.

ERNST: (*Looking at the boots on the table and the dress on the coat hanger*) She didn't take these.

(*He takes the boots off the table and places them carefully on the floor beneath the dress. He sits down, pulls up a chair for* SACHA.)

Sit down here.

(SACHA *sits.*)

You see, now, don't you, you have to leave.

SACHA: (*Head bowed*) I'll wait for her.

ERNST: Yes, in Leningrad.

SACHA: No, I'll wait here. And you?

ERNST: I've a bed at the hospital.

SACHA: If I stay, you'll have a home every night.

ERNST: (*Sceptically*) A home?

SACHA: (*Drily*) It's something, isn't it?

(ERNST *puts his head between his hands and sobs.* SACHA *looks at him for a moment and then, out of tact, tiptoes into his room, leaving the door open. We see the light by his bedside through the door. Mechanism of clock . . .* ERNST *raises his head.*)

ERNST: Sacha . . . Sacha.

(*He looks around the room. Gets up slowly. Puts the chair back under the table. Walks – limping more obviously than usual – towards Sacha's door.*)

I don't want to disturb you.

SACHA: 'I don't want to disturb you.' Sometimes you make me laugh, Ernst Moisseevitch!

(ERNST *enters Sacha's room. From now on we hear their voices but do not see them. The lights in the main room go down. Only the light in Sacha's room remains.*)

ERNST: Tomorrow you must put your name down for the school. You know where it is?

SACHA: Yes, I know.

ERNST: You must send a telegram to your aunt.

SACHA: We must get her winter boots repaired.

ERNST: I'll take them with me tonight. Take care of the money – it should be enough for three months.

SACHA: We'll take great care . . .

(*The image of the 'imagined' family photo – Dacha, Ernst, Sacha – taken during the first scene of this act, is projected on to the twelve square metres of hardboard, the walls of Sacha's room. At first the image is out of focus, gradually it sharpens, as the light through the doorway diminishes. The sharp image is held for twenty seconds before the lights go down.*)